Praise for the Book

'Drawing from the wellsprings of Indic wisdom and personal experience, this book gently yet powerfully guides the reader from confusion to clarity. A heartfelt and inspiring read.'

—Ashwin Sanghi
Bestselling author of *The Krishna Key*, *Chanakya's Chant*, and *The Vault of Vishnu*

'A soul-stirring guide that helps one rise above inner turmoil and discover lasting clarity through the eternal wisdom of India's sacred epics.'

—Dr Anand Ranganathan
Author and scientist

'In the long search for "dharma", individuals from being a "*jignasu*" [enquirer] need to become a *dharmekaa* [a conscious practitioner of dharma]. Shri Punit has beautifully brought out this essence in his book. It is a definitive guide that would help any individual, from being merely curious to becoming truly enquiring.'

—Professor V. Kamakoti
Director, IIT Madras

FROM DOUBT *to* DHARMA

Finding Stillness and Strength through the Teachings of the Ramayana, Mahabharata, and Upanishads

PUNEET SHARMA

HAY HOUSE

HAY HOUSE INDIA
New Delhi • London • Sydney
Carlsbad, California • New York City

Hay House Publishers (India) Pvt Ltd
Muskaan Complex, Plot No. 3, B-2, Vasant Kunj, New Delhi – 110070, India

Hay House LLC, P.O. Box 5100, Carlsbad, CA 92018-5100, USA
Hay House UK Ltd, 1st Floor, Crawford Corner, 91-93 Baker Street, London W1U 6QQ, UK
Hay House Australia Publishing Pty Ltd, 18/36 Ralph St., Alexandria NSW 2015, Australia

Email: contact@hayhouse.co.in
Website: www.hayhouse.co.in

First published by Hay House India, 2025
10 9 8 7 6 5 4 3 2 1

ISBN 978-93-6611-067-7 (Paperback)
ISBN 978-93-6611-802-4 (Ebook)

Printed at Replika Press Pvt Ltd

MIX
Paper | Supporting responsible forestry
FSC www.fsc.org FSC™ C016779

Hay House is committed to a sustainable future for our business, our readers and our planet. This book is made from Forest Stewardship Council® certified paper.

To my late father, Shri Prakash K. Sharma,
who opened my eyes to the wisdom of ancient scriptures
and taught me to read them with faith and reverence.

To my spiritual guru, who showed me the power of silence
and helped me discover the strength that lies within.

To the eternal divine, Lord Krishna, whose timeless smile
inspires me to walk through every phase of life with
calmness, courage, and wisdom held close to the soul.

Contents

Foreword

By Shri Piyush Goyal, Minister of Commerce & Industry
Government of India

I am delighted to learn about the book titled *From Doubt to Dharma* being published by Professor Puneet Sharma. Arriving at a time marked by rapid transformation and deep societal reflection, this work offers timely guidance for those seeking clarity, courage, and purpose in their personal and professional lives.

In an era where individuals are often caught between overwhelming choices and competing demands, the search for steady ground has become increasingly important. The book thoughtfully explores this universal journey, from uncertainty to self-assurance, from hesitation to dharma, anchoring insights in lived experience and philosophical reflection. The book's core message is simple yet powerful: Fearless living is not about eliminating doubt, but about engaging with it meaningfully and aligning one's actions with deeper values and a sense of duty.

Drawing upon India's rich spiritual and intellectual heritage, the book bridges ancient wisdom with modern relevance, encouraging readers to reflect, reassess and reconnect with their own guiding principles while confronting doubts, fears and challenges with greater confidence. The result is a compelling invitation to introspection and growth, resonating with a wide audience, from students and young professionals to seasoned leaders navigating change.

I congratulate Professor Puneet Sharma on this meaningful contribution and hope this book serves as a companion for many in their quest to live more fearlessly and with greater purpose.

Preface

This book is not just written with words that we hear or read in everyday life. It is not only meant to inspire or encourage readers to feel motivated. Every chapter in this book is based on real experiences—those that I have personally gone through, with the grace of my Guru and the quiet strength that came from within.

These are not ideas collected from outside, but thoughts that were born out of pain, mistakes, confusion, and silent learning. Like many others, I, too, have struggled with inner restlessness, overthinking, comparison, fear, and emotional imbalance. At times, I felt lost and unsure, even when things looked fine from the outside. But slowly, and with blessings, I began to see where the real answers lie.

This book is my humble effort to share those truths that helped me. It is not about giving advice but offering simple reflections that may help you connect with your own journey. The wisdom of Dharma, which I found in the Ramayana, the Mahabharata, the Upanishads, the Puranas, and in tiny moments of daily life, showed me a new way of living—more peaceful, more balanced, and more meaningful.

My only wish is that this book becomes useful to you in some small or big way, and that it helps you see your inner patterns, understand your emotions, and take a step towards clarity and self-awareness. There are no quick solutions inside these pages. But if you are willing to reflect and walk honestly, you may slowly discover the power that already lives within you.

This path, from doubt to Dharma, is not about perfection. It is about moving forward with courage and calmness. I offer these words to you, not as a teacher, but as a fellow traveller.

1

Force of Smriti

A Double-Edged Sword

स्मृतिः सत्यवती नित्यं, ज्ञानमूलं शुभाश्रयम्।
सा हि मोक्षाय बन्धाय, यथा भावोनुसारितः॥

One of the most profound shlokas described in Vedantic and yogic philosophy, which signifies *Smriti* (memory) as always truthful and eternal, rooted in wisdom and auspicious refuge. It leads either to liberation or bondage, depending on how it is perceived and followed. If one clings to past regrets, it becomes a chain; if one learns from it, it becomes a path to enlightenment.

Memory, or Smriti, is the fundamental identity of being human. It is vast, limitless, and beyond the grasp of one's imagination. It holds the power to transport a person across time in a mere second.

A single thought can bring back the fragrance of childhood, the laughter of old friendships, or the echoes of long-forgotten pain. It is a silent companion, appearing unexpectedly at any stage of life, unbound by age or circumstance. A person in their final years may suddenly relive a school-day incident as vividly as if it happened yesterday.

But why do we have memory? What is its true purpose? The answer lies in the choices it offers.

Memory is not just a collection of past events filled with sorrow or hatred. It should be a space where we keep joyful moments, lessons we have learnt, values we choose to live by, and promises that help us lead a life of purpose and meaning; it is the most powerful force, a silent superpower that can shape the present life and influence the future. But like all great powers, it must be used with care and attention. When memory is used with wisdom, it becomes a source of strength. It reminds us of valuable lessons, moral values, and the path of own Dharma (the path of righteousness and duty). It helps us grow, avoid repeating mistakes, and live life with a deeper understanding. However, when memory turns into an emotional trap filled with guilt, grief, regrets, or past wounds, it becomes a burden. Instead of guiding us, it controls us. Those who use memory to reflect and rise become stronger, while those who cling to it in sorrow find themselves stuck in pain. The same memory that can lift a person to wisdom can also pull them down into suffering. It all depends on how it is held and used.

People often associate memory with academic learning, memorising facts, theories, definitions, formulas and concepts to secure good grades. But in reality, memory is far more significant. It is not just about recalling information for an exam but about remembering the principles that define our existence. It is the sacred storehouse of knowledge, wisdom, and experiences that shape human character.

Through memory, humanity evolves, adapts, and progresses. Life's most crucial lessons—values, techniques, principles, morals, and rules—are all embedded in memory, helping us navigate an ever-changing world.

For some, memory is a pillar of strength. They remember their values and stand by them, regardless of the situation. No adversity can shake their belief in humanity, kindness, and integrity. Their memory becomes their guiding light, reminding them of their true purpose and inner strength.

However, for many, memory becomes a source of suffering. They cling to past wounds, dwell on failures, and nourish feelings of guilt and vengeance. Instead of using their memory as a tool for growth, they let it imprison them in the past, suffocating their present and clouding their future.

Ideally, only positive and uplifting experiences should reside in one's memory. But can anyone truly control memory? It cannot be erased at will, nor can it be selectively altered.

Over time, through the mastery of the mind, one can learn to filter what deserves attention. The mind is the operator of memory, yet it is often filled with hesitation, confusion, and duality. However, it can be controlled through ancient techniques.

When asked to recall something good, people struggle to remember details. When asked to complain about someone, they recall every detail with absolute clarity. Why? Because they have conditioned themselves to store and retrieve negative experiences more easily than positive ones.

The tendency to remember grievances over gratitude is an unfortunate habit that diminishes the beauty of life.

People often fail to acknowledge the countless small acts of kindness they receive. They remember the grand gestures but overlook the smaller ones, everyday support from those around them. Memory, when misused, becomes transactional, measuring kindness like a trade, rather than cherishing it as a gift.

This is why memory must be consciously shaped to serve one's growth.

A person attending an inspiring session by a great speaker may feel deeply moved, vowing to implement those lessons in life. But if that knowledge is stored only in short-term memory, it fades away quickly, drowned by hesitation and daily distractions. The real challenge lies in making positive memories last and allowing them to influence one's actions in the long run.

Now, imagine a world where humans had no memory. What would life be like? Perhaps, humanity would be freer, happier, and more at peace. Without the weight of past regrets and worries about the future, each person would live fully in the present moment, no burdens, no guilt, no fear, just the beauty of now. Would that be a blessing or a loss? That is a question only memory itself can answer using its wisdom accumulated over the years.

Memory is a strange force, powerful enough to shape destinies, yet delicate enough to be swayed by the choices one makes.

The Mandukya Upanishad explains memory through three states of consciousness: Waking (*Jagrat*), dreaming (*Swapna*), and deep sleep (*Sushupti*). In the waking state, memory is active but influenced by intellectual logic, shaped by past impressions, and operated by the ego, which leads to hesitation in accepting the unknown and unseen truth. It retains knowledge selectively, often reinforcing personal biases rather than truth. In the dreaming state, Smriti operates freely, unbound by reason, allowing suppressed emotions and subconscious impressions to surface. It offers insights but remains unpredictable, blending reality with illusion. In deep sleep, memory becomes dormant, and the self exists beyond thought and perception. It is a state of pure rest, free from desires and impressions, leaving behind only an experience of true peace.

The Yoga Sutras of Patanjali (1.11) define Smriti as the retention of past experiences. This retention, however, is not limited to a single lifetime but extends across births, explaining why individuals exhibit unexplainable fears, talents, or inclinations from an early age.

Most of us don't live truly; we only serve the mind, which turns us into slaves of our own Smriti.

In most cases, memory serves as a greater source of revenge than of joy. If someone insults us, we do not just remember their face but also their words, the exact situation, the place, the date, and even the time it happened. Every detail is recorded in our minds as if engraved on stone. But when it comes to cherishing something beautiful, an act of kindness, a moment of love, a lesson of wisdom, we often struggle to recall such fine details.

Why does the mind function this way? The answer lies in the interplay of ego, choice, and hesitation. Ego magnifies wounds, making them unforgettable. Choice decides whether one holds on to pain or lets it go. Hesitation fuels negativity, preventing one from taking the right action at the right time.

A hesitant mind lingers in doubt, constantly analysing, yet failing to move forward. Instead of bringing peace, memory becomes a burden that keeps a person trapped in cycles of regret and resentment.

History and scriptures bear witness to how memory, when misused, can lead even the greatest warriors and scholars astray. Karna, one of the most valiant and generous warriors, carried the weight of his past insult throughout his life. The memory of being rejected because of his caste haunted him so deeply that it dictated his choices. Instead of rising above it, he chose to align with Duryodhana despite knowing he was fighting on the side of *Adharma*. He had the opportunity to change his path when Lord Krishna himself offered him guidance, but he remained bound by his wounded memory.

This choice did not just cost him his life; it also took away his credibility, making him an instrument of destruction rather than the great hero he could have been.

On the other hand, Ravana, the mighty king of Lanka, was another victim of his own memory. Instead of letting go of the insult his sister, Shurpanakha, suffered at the hands of Lakshman, he let it consume him. His memory of that humiliation turned into an obsession for revenge, pushing him towards Adharma. That one act of vengeance, born out of a memory he refused to erase, led to the destruction of his empire, his lineage, and ultimately, his own life. Had he chosen to rise above his memory instead of acting on it, perhaps history would have been different.

Conversely, those who chose to fill their memories with wisdom and positivity found a path to greatness. Vidura, the most intelligent and righteous advisor of King Dhritarashtra, was born to a lower-caste mother. He could have let that fact dictate his life, allowing resentment to cloud his mind. But instead of dwelling on his birth, he made the choice to embrace knowledge and wisdom. He chose to stand on the side of Dharma. He studied the Shastras, lived by the highest principles of Dharma, and became the guiding force behind the Kuru dynasty. His memory did not weigh him down; it lifted him towards wisdom and righteousness.

Sugriva, too, faced an insult at the hands of Lakshman. When Lord Ram sought his help in finding Sita, Sugriva had promised his support. But after gaining his kingdom, he became lost in comfort and pleasure and forgot his promise. When Lakshman arrived to remind him, he did so harshly, insulting Sugriva in front of his own people. Any other king, bound by ego, might have reacted with rage. But Sugriva did not let his memory turn into resentment. Instead, he chose to recall his promise and correct his mistake. Without hesitation, he gathered his army and devoted himself to fulfilling his duty towards Ram. His memory could have been a source of anger, but he transformed it into a source of righteousness and duty to stand along with Dharma.

Moreover, Kunti, the mother of the Pandavas, was a woman of great strength, but her life was filled with struggles. She had to endure the memory of giving away her firstborn son, Karna, and later witness the suffering of her five sons in exile. Despite all this, Kunti used her memory wisely—she never let sorrow weaken her spirit. She taught her sons the value of patience, Dharma, and humility. Even after the war, when she revealed the truth about Karna, she remembered the need for peace rather than lamenting her past mistake.

This is the power of memory; it does not control us unless we allow it to. It can lead to downfall or greatness, depending on what one chooses to remember and how one chooses to act upon it. If people only stored wisdom, kindness, and positivity in their memories, they would never be bound by hatred and revenge. But if they cling to insults, wounds, and regrets, they will always find themselves trapped in the past, unable to move forward.

One of my friends is a clear example of how Smriti, or the grip of memory, can quietly disturb a person's peace. He holds on to every small incident from the past as if it just happened. He still remembers the exact date, time, and place of a relative's wedding where he was not called on stage to take a photo with the bride and groom. He often brings up how his office boy once ignored serving him afternoon tea, and he speaks about it as if it were a deep personal insult.

He proudly shares the story of how he helped a fellow passenger who forgot his bag on the train. He narrates it with such pride, believing it to be a great act of kindness. Once, he gave a small donation to a beggar, and now he often refers to it when advising others to donate, as if that one act gives him moral authority. Every time we speak to him, he starts recounting everything that happened since the last time we talked. His stories are all from the past, and it feels like he is more comfortable living in old memories than embracing the present. Without realising it, he has chosen to remain in Smriti, using the past as a shelter while the present quietly slips away. It is not wrong to remember, but when we keep repeating the past, we forget to live fully in the now.

Perhaps memories are meant to guide us, not to govern us. When we carry every small hurt or victory from the past into the present, we unknowingly fill our today with yesterday's weight. Life moves forward, but we remain stuck. Real growth begins when we learn to honour the past without living in it. Let the lessons stay but allow the pain and pride to leave as well. The present is not a stage for replaying old stories; it is a fresh page waiting for new experiences. To truly live, we must step out of the shadows of Smriti and walk with awareness into the light of now.

The greatest lesson memory teaches is that it's not the past that defines who we are, but the choices we make in response to it.

The past cannot be changed, but the way we remember and use it can shape our present and future. The wise ones remember what uplifts them, and the lost ones remember what destroys them.

The deletion of memory does not happen through force or resistance; rather, it begins with the simple act of avoidance and overlooking. Just as hesitation causes us to overlook opportunities that could change our lives, we must learn to overlook the past, regrets, and painful memories that serve no purpose except to hold us back.

The mind is a subtle and intelligent entity; it follows the patterns we create. If we repeatedly dwell on negative memories, it assumes they are important and keeps bringing them back, much like a music app that tracks our preferences and suggests similar songs we listen to the most.

Every time we revisit a regretful moment or a painful event, we reinforce its importance, making it harder to forget. However, if we consistently ignore and overlook such memories, the mind begins to notice that they are no longer relevant. Over time, it slowly removes them from its primary storage, pushing them further into the background, until they eventually lose their grip on us.

This is not a process of suppression but of right redirection. Instead of fighting to erase a memory, one must replace it with something more meaningful, just as we replace a song on our playlist when our preferences change. The mind operates on familiarity—whatever we give attention to, it amplifies; whatever we disregard, it diminishes.

By consciously choosing to overlook the past, refusing to engage in regrets, choosing to stand on the side of Dharma and shifting focus towards growth, joy, and learning, we can reprogramme the mind to store useful Smriti and recall only what truly matters. In this manner, memory becomes a tool of empowerment rather than a burden of suffering and doubts.

Think about it: You are not tired because of others, but because of the solidity inside you. Let go of the old, bad memories and keep only those that bring peace and add meaning to your life's journey.

In the end, we realise that Smriti doesn't heal, it hurts the most.

Exercise

To truly understand the power of Smriti and its influence on our lives, dedicate two days to this simple yet profound exercise.

Day 1: Reflect on and relive all your painful and worst memories, one after the other. No matter how much suffering it brings, allow yourself to experience the unnecessary pain created by Smriti in this moment, pain that has no real connection with the present. Observe your mood, emotions, and your mind's stability.

Day 2: Shift your focus and recall all the positive, joyful, and cherished memories. Compare your emotions, mindset, and overall approach to life between these two days. Notice the stark difference in your mood and perspective.

You may feel a longing to relive the joy of the second day, but the key takeaway is to recognise how Smriti has the power to shape your thoughts either positively or negatively, either discouraging or uplifting you.

Through this exercise, you will not only intellectually understand Smriti but will also directly experience its impact on your life and inner self.

Key Takeaways

We have been given a special gift called Smriti. It helps us remember the good moments in life, the promises we make to ourselves, the values we choose to follow, and the lessons that keep us clear and focused. However, many a time, under the control of our thoughts and emotions created by the mind, we use this gift in the wrong manner. Instead of remembering what makes us strong, we store hurt, insults, failures, anger, and wrong ideas. Slowly, this beautiful power starts working against us instead of helping us.

Therefore, the person who uses Smriti as a tool for hope, learning, and positive thinking is the one who truly lives a happy and meaningful life. When memory is used with wisdom, it helps us grow stronger, stay focused, and build a healthy way of thinking. But for those who don't understand how to use it well, life becomes a repeated list of failures, waiting to be filled.

2
The Myth of Multitasking
Focus Divided Is Focus Lost

व्यसनेषु मनोपि धैर्यमनुज्ञा, स्थिरमतिर्जयति।

One of the most profound shlokas from the Mahabharata, Udyoga Parva (43.2), elaborates that even in the face of difficulties, the one who possesses unwavering focus, and a steady mind emerges victorious.

The world we live in today is constantly racing ahead. People prepare themselves for multitasking, believing it to be a necessity of time, both in their personal and professional lives. Society glorifies those who can juggle multiple tasks simultaneously, praising their efficiency and speed. The corporate world rewards those who claim to be excellent multitaskers, and even at home, individuals pride themselves on managing several activities simultaneously.

But here lies a fundamental truth: Multitasking is a myth. At times, it goes against the teachings of the Dharma. It is an illusion, an idea that has evolved over time due to the growing pressures of survival, competition, and the never-ending chase for achievements. People have convinced themselves that doing multiple things at once is a sign of intelligence and efficiency. But in reality, multitasking is nothing more than a deception that weakens our ability to focus (*Ekagrata*) and truly excel in the core areas.

To understand this, let's perform a simple activity. First, try speaking the English alphabet from A to Z. You will notice that you can say it smoothly without hesitation. Now, count from 1 to 26. Once again, the task is effortless. But now, attempt to do both together, say, 'A-1, B-2, C-3, D-4 and so on.' Within a few seconds, you will realise that it is hard to maintain the same flow. Most people struggle to go beyond H-8 without slowing down or making mistakes. Why does this happen? Because the mind does not work efficiently when forced to switch between two different tasks. It struggles to divide attention, making even simple tasks unnecessarily complex.

Some might argue here that with enough practise, multitasking can become easier with this task as well. However, many people don't realise that while practise helps us improve, it works only because we focus fully on one task at a time. We don't multitask while practising, we give our complete attention to that activity. That is the real strength of Ekagrata: Focusing on one task at a time, rather than multitasking.

In the modern world, multitasking is often perceived as a valuable skill that enhances efficiency, productivity, and intelligence. People believe that handling multiple tasks simultaneously helps them accomplish more in less time. However, research presented by the American Psychological Association has proven that multitasking is a cognitive illusion; the brain does not truly perform multiple tasks at once but rather switches rapidly between them. This constant shifting leads to reduced efficiency, increased errors, and heightened mental fatigue. Neuroscience reveals that the human brain is designed for managing single tasks. The prefrontal cortex, the part of the brain responsible for decision-making and focus, can handle only one complex task at a time. When a person tries to multitask, the brain rapidly switches between tasks rather than processing them simultaneously. This is a pure form of *Chanchalta* (fickleness).

History and spirituality have always emphasised the power of singular focus. The Mahabharata provides us with the perfect example through the story of Arjun. When Guru Dronacharya tested his students by asking them to aim at a bird's eye, he questioned each of them about what they saw. Some mentioned the tree, the branches, the sky, and even the bird's body. But when Arjun was asked, his answer was simple: I see only the bird's eye. That was the power of his focus. While the others were distracted by everything around them, Arjun had trained his mind without any hesitation to concentrate (Ekagra) on only one goal at a time. This unwavering attention is what made him the greatest archer of his time. The rest of the Pandavas and Kauravas were unknowingly multitasking by paying attention to various elements around them, while Arjun, with his laser-like focus, remained undeterred.

Focus is like rain—when directed, it nurtures; when wasted, it floods.

The illusion of multitasking affects almost everyone in their daily lives. People talk on the phone while driving, read while making notes, cook while watching television, and work on computers with multiple tabs open at once. They assume that they are successfully managing everything, but in reality, their efficiency drops. A driver talking on the phone is far more likely to be in an accident. A cook distracted by a television show may spoil the dish. A student reading and writing at the same time may fail to grasp the depth of knowledge contained in the words. These activities give a false sense of productivity, but the truth is that multitasking only divides attention and reduces effectiveness.

Over time, as people repeat the same set of daily activities, their minds become accustomed to handling them in an automated manner. A biker controls the handle, changes gear, keeps his foot on the brake, and moves through chaotic traffic. It may seem like multitasking, but in reality, it is simply muscle memory taking over. The moment an unexpected or sudden obstacle appears, a biker who is also talking on the phone is more likely to crash.

Yet, despite these realities, people fail to recognise the deception of multitasking. Parents unknowingly push their children into this illusion from an early age, enrolling them in multiple activities—school, sports, hobbies, cultural activities and competitions—all at once. They believe they are preparing their children for a competitive world, but they are, in fact, burdening young minds with divided focus.

The pressure to perform well in everything leads to stress, anxiety, and burnout. Instead of excelling in one field with complete dedication and focus, children grow up trying to balance too many things without mastering any in a pure form of doubt or hesitation.

Even adults get caught in this habit. Many people keep multitasking because, deep down, they feel they are not doing one thing well enough. So, they keep switching to other tasks, hoping to do better there. That's why many employees seek transfers instead of promotions, and even business owners keep changing their products or services, because they struggle to focus on improving just one thing.

Here, Maharshi Patanjali, the great sage of yoga, taught that the key to self-realisation lies in Ekagrata (the art of focusing), the power of one-pointed concentration. His Yoga Sutras explain that a restless mind, scattered in many directions, can never attain true wisdom. But when the mind is steady, deeply focused like an unwavering flame, it rises beyond ordinary consciousness and reaches a state of pure awareness, the direction of Dharma itself.

The entire concept of multitasking was not a natural human ability; it was sold to people by a few enthusiastic corporate trainers, motivational speakers, and self-proclaimed productivity experts. These individuals needed to bring something 'new' to their audience, and so they glorified multitasking as a skill to be mastered. Becoming an expert in multitasking became a trend, and people who were always looking for shortcuts to success embraced it without question. They believed that performing two tasks simultaneously was better than doing them separately, assuming it would save time and effort. However, in the process, they failed to see that multitasking does not produce high-quality results; it only creates an illusion of efficiency.

True success comes from focus (Ekagrata) with competency and alignment to Dharma, not from scattering attention (Chanchalta) across multiple tasks. Those who achieve greatness in any field, be it art, science, business, or spirituality, do so by dedicating themselves wholeheartedly to their craft. A musician does not compose a masterpiece while checking e-mails. A scientist does not make groundbreaking discoveries while scrolling through social media. A spiritual seeker does not attain enlightenment while engaging in worldly distractions. Every great achievement has been the result of deep, undivided focus rooted in Dharma.

The time has come to break the illusion of multitasking. It is time to return to the wisdom of the Ekagrata, to follow the path of Arjun, to dedicate ourselves fully to one task at a time. In doing so, we will not only enhance our productivity but also bring clarity, commitment, and excellence into our efforts and eliminate the deeper doubts from our minds.

In our daily lives, we often find ourselves engaged in conversations where we pretend to listen while our minds are busy framing the next question or response. It is a common habit, something almost everyone does without even realising it. But have we ever wondered why, after such conversations, we struggle to recall what was actually said? Why do we often feel disconnected, unable to fully grasp the essence of the discussion? The answer lies in the silent yet powerful enemy—multitasking.

When we listen to someone speak, our mind should ideally be calm, open, and fully present. But instead, it is restless, jumping ahead, already crafting a reply before the other person has even finished their sentence. This is where we lose the depth of the conversation. In trying to do two things at once, listening and thinking, we do neither effectively.

This habit is not just limited to casual conversations. It extends to meetings, lectures, and even spiritual discourses. Many people attend speeches and sermons, yet their minds wander. They are physically present, but mentally elsewhere, half-listening, half-thinking about what to ask next, or even worse, planning their next task for the day. They believe they are engaging, but in reality, they are only hearing, not listening.

Words are not just sounds or letters. They carry feelings. They can lift someone's heart or break it. They have the power to set a person free or tie them down. Some words bring hope, and others can deeply hurt. It all depends on how we choose to speak. When we use words, we must try to spread kindness, not pain. Sentences should bring joy, not sorrow.

Knowing the wrong, yet choosing it—that's not weakness, that's betrayal of the self.

In the great epics, this truth is beautifully illustrated. When Lord Krishna spoke the Bhagavad Gita to Arjun, Arjun was not framing his next question while listening. He was completely immersed (Ekagra) in Krishṇa's words, surrendering his mind and heart to divine wisdom. If he had engaged in mental multitasking or doubts, he would have lost the essence of the Gita, missing the life-changing guidance that it offered.

In today's fast-paced world, this art of Ekagrata, rooted in Dharma, is fading. We are so eager to speak, to respond, to prove our point that we do not truly listen. We assume that by forming quick replies, we are being efficient. But we disconnect from the depth of conversation in doing so.

We choose thinking over focus, and that's the mind's greatest game.

As you read this book, take a moment to observe your mind. Have you stayed with every word, absorbing the essence of what is being conveyed? Or have you wandered to distant thoughts, perhaps recalling an old memory, planning the next task of the day, connecting a topic with other people or wondering about something entirely unrelated? Even as your eyes move from one word to the next, reading in a flow, your mind has likely been travelling elsewhere, jumping from one thought to another.

This is how the human mind works, constantly shifting, rarely still, always seeking to do more than one thing at a time. It is this very nature of the mind that gives birth to the illusion of multitasking.

In the wisdom of ancient teachings, it has always been said that a task must be done with complete presence. Whether it is work, worship, study, or even the simplest of daily chores, one must dedicate oneself fully to it. When the body is engaged in action, the mind should also be aligned with that action. It is this singular focus that brings efficiency, peace, and excellence in everything one does.

However, in reality, it moves in the opposite direction. Modern workplaces glorify multitasking. A single employee is expected to handle multiple responsibilities, switch between different tasks without a pause, and still be efficient. Bosses take pride in pushing their teams towards multitasking, believing it to be the hallmark of productivity. But is it truly productive? Look around the corporate world today; do we see a rise in happiness, satisfaction, or excellence? Debatable and doubtful! Instead, we surely see growing stress, mental fatigue, and declining quality of work.

The truth is, when a person is engaged in one task but is forced to think of another, the mind becomes divided (Chanchal). It neither focuses entirely on the task at hand nor properly plans for the next. The outcome is half-hearted work, incomplete understanding, increasing hesitation, and rising dissatisfaction. That is why, despite long working hours and endless meetings, so many workplaces struggle with inefficiency. People are busy, but they are not effective. They work more but achieve less. Their attention is scattered, their creativity is blocked, and their sense of fulfilment is nearly lost.

The mind always tries to keep us busy with one thought or another, one act or the next. It is its nature to stay engaged and to pull us into multiple things at once. As shared earlier, when we are listening to someone, it creates unrelated thoughts. While eating, it drifts away to some different place. When we are sitting silently, it takes us either into the future or the past. This habit of doing many things at once, this restlessness, often emerges in our daily actions, too. But pause for a moment and reflect: Can anyone truly enjoy their food if they are not mentally present? Can a person sit in peace with wandering thoughts? The truth is, when two acts are done at the same time, neither one is done properly. That's why many people struggle to focus deeply or become experts in one thing. And that's where the old saying comes alive, 'Too many cooks spoil the broth!'

The pages of ancient epics and sacred texts whisper the same eternal wisdom of dharma and Ekagrata. Eklavya, the warrior of the Mahabharata, possessed no royal lineage, no privilege of an esteemed guru's guidance. Yet, his unwavering devotion to practice, his consistency and singular focus made him an archer even greater than Arjun himself.

One of the deepest reasons why many of us struggle to stay consistent or fully devoted to a single goal is our quiet impatience. We are often in a hurry to reach the destination, forgetting that the true beauty lies in the journey itself. In our rush for quick results, we overlook the power of steady effort and the quiet strength of perseverance. We chase outcomes, hoping success will come swiftly, yet ignore the foundation it is built upon—focused effort, daily discipline, and a mind open to learning. Mastery does not come from doing everything at once; it comes from doing one thing well, again and again, with purpose and passion.

Look around, and the world itself whispers the secret of perseverance. A mere drop of water, falling with unwavering consistency, can carve its way through the hardest stone. A trickle, when persistent, can transform into a mighty river, a river that in time embraces the vastness of the ocean. In the same way, every great achievement, every remarkable feat, is not born from sudden bursts of effort but from the focused, undoubted discipline of consistency.

The Chandogya Upanishad describes how deep Ekagrata leads to self-realisation, just as a lamp flame remains steady in a windless place without a doubt.

A story from the Purana elaborates this concept in a wider context—of King Jivala, a powerful ruler known for his sharp mind and strategic brilliance. His court was filled with ministers who admired his ability to listen to multiple people at once, write letters, and plan wars simultaneously. He took great pride in being a multitasker, believing that it made him more capable than other kings. One day, an enemy kingdom launched a sudden attack. Jivala was in a meeting discussing trade policies, while also reviewing taxation documents and responding to a messenger about a festival celebration. In his desire to handle everything at once, he only half-listened to the war alert. He quickly ordered his army to defend the eastern border, assuming that's where the attack originated.

However, the enemy had actually invaded from the western border. By the time Jivala realised his mistake, the city had already been plundered. His greatest strength, his ability to handle multiple things at once, had become his biggest weakness. The army was scattered, decisions were made in haste, and in the end, he lost the battle due to his divided attention.

Similarly, the story of transformation finds its most remarkable example in Valmiki. Once a feared bandit, lost in the darkness of ignorance, he discovered his true self through the power of deep meditation, unwavering focus, and devotion to Lord Ram. Guided by dharma and with complete Ekagrata, he immersed himself in penance so deeply that it transformed his very nature. From a man once known for violence, he became a sage respected by all. His focused journey gave birth to the

Ramayana, an epic so timeless and profound that it continues to guide and inspire millions.

Perhaps, Ekagrata is like a mango tree. It takes time to grow, but when it bears fruit, the results are sweet and fulfilling. On the other hand, Chanchalta is like a bitter gourd vine, which grows quickly and shows results early, but what it gives is full of bitterness.

Exercise

This exercise will help you realise how a divided mind struggles to absorb information and why deep focus is necessary for true understanding.

Task 1: Pick a random paragraph from any book or article. While reading, check your phone notifications or listen to music with lyrics. After finishing the paragraph, close the book and try to summarise what you just read.

You will likely remember very little or recall it incorrectly because your mind was divided while multitasking.

Task 2: Pick another paragraph from the same book or article. This time, switch off your phone, find a quiet place, and read it with complete focus. After reading, close the book and mentally summarise the content.

Notice how much better you remember the details and how the words make more sense when your attention is undivided or, perhaps, in Ekagrata.

This simple test will show that when the mind is doing two things at once, it absorbs neither of them properly. But when fully present (Ekagrata) in one task, it processes information deeply and meaningfully.

Key Takeaways

This chapter emphasises the significance of focus, highlighting the importance of dedicating oneself to one task at a time rather than getting caught in the illusion of multitasking, which is neither productive nor enriching. Hesitation often leads people to multitask out of the fear that focusing on a single task might be a waste of time. However, in reality, dividing attention between two activities does not save time; it results in wasted effort, diminished experience, and reduced efficiency.

3

Shraddha in Saburi

The Essence of Manifestation

श्रद्धामयोऽयं पुरुषो यो यच्छ्रद्धः स एव सः ॥

ONE OF THE MOST PROFOUND SHLOKAS ON *SHRADDHA* (FAITH) originates from the Bhagavad Gita (17.3). It states that a person is shaped by their faith; whatever they deeply believe in, they eventually become. This verse emphasises that faith is not just a belief but a powerful force that influences thoughts, actions, and character, ultimately shaping one's destiny.

The Atharvaveda (19.42.1) prays, Shraddha (faith) is the first essence of life. As per the Mundaka Upanishad, faith is the gateway to knowledge and liberation.

One of the finest examples of true faith comes from the story of young devotee Prahlad. Even as a child, he believed with all his heart that his God, Lord Vishnu, would protect him, no matter what form He would have to take. Prahlad's father, the powerful demon king Hiranyakashipu, was against his devotion. He tried to kill him many times, simply because he was worshipping Lord Vishnu. The king had received a strange boon—he could not be killed by any man or woman, not by an animal or bird, not during the day or night, not inside or outside the house, and not by any weapon. Still, Prahlad never lost his faith. His Shraddha remained strong, and because of that, Lord Vishnu appeared in the fierce form of Narasimha, half-man, half-lion, and found a unique way to end the evil. He appeared at twilight, neither day nor night, on the doorstep, neither inside nor outside, and used His claws, not any weapon, to kill the evil. This tale is not just about divine intervention, but about what unshaken faith can bring.

In today's world, such Shraddha is rare. People often say they have faith—faith in themselves, in their dreams, in their loved ones, but when challenges come, they quickly start seeking approval from others, doubting their own path, and looking for shortcuts. Their shraddha becomes conditional and temporary. They keep shifting their faith based on situations, sometimes on efforts, sometimes on luck, and often on the opinions of others. True shraddha is constant, not something that changes with circumstances.

Without Shraddha, one cannot truly understand the meaning of Saburi, which is patience. Patience is not just about waiting; it is about remaining calm, steady, and full of faith during the wait. It is the quiet strength to endure uncertainty without losing trust. When Shraddha and Saburi come together, the mind becomes peaceful, actions become meaningful, and life begins to flow in alignment with true dharma.

Where Shraddha is true, Saburi follows silently.

Together, they help a person reach their true potential and lead to real growth and success. But in today's fast-moving world, everyone wants quick results. People are in such a hurry that if they could, they would want to deliver a child before nine months, they would plant a seed in the morning and hope for a tree with ripe fruits by evening, they would join a gym on

Monday and look for six-pack abs by Sunday, and they would pray once and ask the universe to rearrange its plan for them. But life doesn't work that way. The lack of patience and deep faith has made us restless and disconnected from the natural process of growth.

Shraddha is not just for devotion to God. It is needed in every aspect of life, whether it is personal goals, relationships, health, success, or spiritual growth. At the same time, Saburi is the strength to keep going, even when results are not visible or favourable. Together, they teach us to trust the process and believe that everything will fall into place at the right time, in alignment with dharma.

What money is to humans, Shraddha is to the divine.

Faith is not something that someone else can place inside us; it does not come from fabricated words or an order from Amazon. True Shraddha rises from within, from the silent corners of the heart and the calm spaces of the mind, when we allow it to nourish. It begins the moment we start trusting ourselves, our strength, our hidden potential, and the inner voice that tells us, 'You can!' When this inner belief becomes strong, it gently pushes us forward, helping us take steps without being scared of falling or being judged. The one who walks with Shraddha does not get trapped in endless thoughts or confused by too many opinions. The mind stays light, the focus clear, and the path slowly begins to appear. And with each step taken in faith, the soul starts learning the art of Saburi, the patience to wait, to grow, and to bloom. Doubts, which once looked so loud and real, begin to fade away on their own, like mist disappearing in morning light.

In the timeless tales of Hindu mythology, Shraddha has always been the force that clears the fog of doubt and awakens hidden strength. When Lord Hanuman stood at the edge of the vast ocean, preparing to search for Sita, a moment of hesitation touched his heart. He wondered if such a leap was even possible. But the moment he remembered who he truly was, and placed his complete faith, his shraddha in Lord Ram, the doubt melted away like darkness before dawn. That inner faith unlocked his forgotten power. With unshaken Shraddha and calm Saburi, he soared across the ocean, not just with strength, but with the clarity of purpose.

Psychologically, Shraddha builds emotional confidence, clears doubts, and allows the mind to focus on possibilities rather than fears. Fear is not just a feeling; it quietly enters the mind and changes everything. Even if our mind holds 90 per cent positivity, just 10 per cent fear can turn it all into negativity. Like one drop of ink in clear water, fear spreads and takes over. It brings confusion, overthinking, hesitation, and constant self-doubt. It drains energy, weakens focus, and kills motivation. A fearful mind stops seeing hope and only notices risk. But Saburi, the quiet strength of patience, fades fear slowly but completely. It gives us calm in chaos, steadiness in storms, and courage in moments of doubt. With Saburi, fear loses its voice, and the mind finds peace again. Together, both Shraddha and Saburi create the inner stability needed for clarity, meaningful decision-making, and ultimate growth. These two virtues are not limited to personal success alone; they breathe life into relationships. In friendships, partnerships, and families, it is shraddha that plants a seed of deep trust, and Saburi that waters those seeds through patience, forgiveness, and understanding. Without these, bonds break under pressure; with them, love matures into an unshakable foundation.

However, when people hear the words 'Shraddha' and 'Saburi', their minds often turn towards religion, rituals, or spiritual practices. Many connect these concepts only with temples, gods, or ancient scriptures. While it's true that these values have been nurtured through sacred texts and spiritual wisdom, their essence goes far beyond the boundaries of belief systems. Shraddha and Saburi are not limited to devotion alone; they are powerful companions in living a peaceful, purposeful, and fulfilling life. Some may feel uncomfortable when these words are linked with ancient texts, as if they belong only to tradition or blind faith. But in reality, these are not about following a particular path; they are about discovering oneself.

Whether one believes in a supreme power, a god, or any form of divinity, Shraddha and Saburi are not tied to such beliefs. These two words are not about worship, rituals, or bowing before anything or anyone; they are about rising within. At their core, they are deeply personal. Shraddha means trusting your inner voice, your actions, your efforts, and your true self. Whereas, Saburi is the quiet strength to continue with patience, even when the world around is rushing, restless, or unclear. These are not teachings that demand surrender; they are reminders to stand tall, to stay rooted in one's truth. They do not ask you to believe in what lies outside, but to believe in what breathes inside. So be selfish in the right way, use these powerful tools not for rituals, but for your upliftment. Don't push them away, thinking they belong only to sacred texts or spiritual traditions. They are timeless, beyond labels, beyond borders. They are companions for anyone who wishes to walk peacefully, purposefully, and powerfully through life with trust in the self and patience in life.

Modern science acknowledges the deep significance of Shraddha and Saburi in shaping a meaningful and balanced life as well. Among the leading voices in this space is Dr Sarah Schnitker, a renowned psychologist at Baylor University, who has brought scientific clarity to the ancient virtue of Saburi. Through her pioneering research, Dr Schnitker has shown that patience is far more than just waiting without complaint. It is an active psychological strength, one that helps individuals manage their emotions, pursue their goals with clarity, and experience a deeper sense of life satisfaction. In doing so, she reveals how Saburi supports mental resilience and helps individuals find purpose, even amidst life's uncertainties and doubts.

Lord Krishna, through his timeless words in the Gita, kept reminding Arjun and all seekers by saying, *Karmanye vadhikaraste ma phaleshu kadachana* [your right is only to perform your actions, never to the fruits of your actions]. In these simple yet profound lines lie the true heart of Shraddha and Saburi: Faith in one's effort and patience in the unseen results. Swami Vivekananda, standing tall before the world in his historic speech in America, echoed the same spirit, urging all to have unwavering faith in themselves and to continue on their path without fear. Rabindranath Tagore captured the soul of shraddha when he said that faith is the bird that feels the light and sings when the dawn is still dark—a trust that does not need proof, but lives on pure belief. In the modern world, visionaries like Elon Musk unknowingly breathe these ancient teachings. His unshaken faith in ideas that once seemed impossible, like autonomous cars and missions to space, and his silent endurance through failures, show how Shraddha and Saburi still rule the foundation of real achievements.

From ancient times to today, these two virtues have been the quiet roots beneath every towering success. They have guided the footsteps of countless souls, from moments of doubt to the discovery of dharma, from restless wandering to purposeful living. They are not just waiting in scriptures or speeches; they are waiting quietly within you, whispering through every heartbeat, asking only to be embraced. If you allow them space in your heart, you, too, can feel lighter, freer, stronger, and truly taste the joy of having real faith in yourself. A faith that does not tremble before storms but rises like a sun within, lighting up your true being.

Saburi questions, Shraddha answers.

Always remember, we are blessed with just this one life, this one breath, and this one precious moment, which is slipping away faster than we realise, like sand flowing through our fingers. Every ticking sound of the clock is not just a reminder of time passing; it is life moving forward. Yet, many of us waste these golden moments by overthinking, doubting too often, and standing still at the doorstep of new possibilities. Fear, hesitation, and confusion silently hold us back. In doing so, we forget that the real loss is not in failing, but in never taking the first step towards our dharma, the path we are meant to walk.

Hold this truth close to your heart: If you plant your efforts with Shraddha and water them every day with Saburi, something beautiful will surely grow. It may not happen today or tomorrow, but the seeds of your faith, patience, and hard work will bloom when the time is right.

Trust the process, trust yourself, and walk ahead with a smiling heart.

Exercise

Imagine discovering Aladdin's lamp with a genie inside. If you had three wishes, what would they be? Write them down:

Wish one: ____
Wish two: ____
Wish three: ____

Now, take a moment to reflect. These wishes represent your deepest priorities and desires. But isn't it ironic that instead of believing in ourselves, we expect a magical genie to fulfil them?

The genie is just a fantasy, an illusion, a form of Maya. Waiting for miracles creates doubt and weakens *Shraddha* (faith) in our own ability to achieve these dreams. The excitement and joy you felt while imagining these wishes, aren't they worth pursuing in real life?

Will excuses, hesitation, and doubt ever bring the same happiness as actually achieving them? Instead of waiting for magic, why not trust in faith, perseverance, and action? Why not take a few more steps, give a few more attempts, this time, with complete faith in yourself?

In this way, one can attain *moksha* (liberation) from doubts and hesitation through self-earned karma, while still alive, within the flow of time and space, guided by the very energy that connects us to our true purpose.

Key Takeaways

This chapter explores the timeless relevance of Shraddha and Saburi as essential inner virtues that go beyond religious or spiritual boundaries. It emphasises that these qualities are not about devotion to external forces but about building a deep trust in oneself and nurturing the strength to wait calmly for outcomes. Shraddha is described as the foundation of self-belief and clarity, while Saburi is the quiet force that sustains focus and calm through life's uncertainties

4

Karma over Maya

Thoughtful Action, Not Illusion

तस्मादसक्तः सततं कार्यं कर्म समाचर।
असक्तो ह्याचरन्कर्म परमाप्नोति पूरुषः॥

One of the most important teachings of the Bhagavad Gita (3.19) is about Nishkama Karma, which means selfless action. In this verse, Lord Krishna advises Arjun to perform his duty with full dedication but without worrying about success or failure. He teaches that when a person works without selfish motives, their actions lead to inner peace and liberation, instead of creating stress or attachment.

On the other hand, the Bhagavata Purana (Canto 11, Chapter 7, Verse 7) explains the concept of Maya (illusion):

मायामयं इदं विश्वं पश्यन् न तत्त्वतो द्विज।
स्वप्नं नाना-विधं दृष्ट्वा नेहाज्ञोऽनुस्मरेद्‌धः॥

This verse tells us that the material world is an illusion created by Maya. Just like a dream feels real when we are sleeping but disappears when we wake up, the world appears real but is actually temporary and always changing. A wise person understands this truth and does not become overly attached to material things, knowing that they are not permanent.

Maya, or illusion, is nothing but a false reality created by misconceptions, assumptions, half-truths, and projections. It arises when a person lacks complete knowledge, doubts the source of wisdom, or hesitates to seek clarity.

Maya is like a dark web that quietly covers the mind and thoughts, wrapping them in false ideas and illusions. It makes a person believe in what is not real, and slowly, the lie starts to feel like the truth. Under this shadow, one begins to think that whatever they know is the only reality. But the real truth is not found in assumptions or surface knowledge; it reveals itself only through deep self-awareness and sincere, consistent practice of one's karma (duties).

Maya is a witch, beauty on the face, poison in the core.

Karma requires action, and anything that prevents a person from doing what is right and necessary in alignment with Dharma is a form of doubt. A great example of this is seen in the Mahabharata during the infamous game of dice. When Yudhishthira kept losing one thing after another, he eventually lost his kingdom, his brothers, and finally, he was about to stake his wife, Draupadi, in the court. Bhishma Pitamah, the wisest and most powerful elder in the Kuru Dynasty, remained silent. He did not stop this injustice, not because he was powerless, but because he hesitated to perform his Dharma and Karma. He was bound by his vow to follow the orders of the King of Hastinapur. This hesitation, this doubt of duty towards an oath, became a burden over his true Karma. His silence allowed the injustice to continue until Draupadi was dragged into the court and humiliated.

This was Maya clouding Karma, causing the mighty Bhishma to forget the higher path of Dharma in the name of his vow. Had Bhishma risen above his inner conflict and spoken out, the devastating war of Kurukshetra might have been avoided. If he had firmly objected to Draupadi's humiliation in the royal court, none would have dared to challenge him. Yet he remained silent, misled by Maya into believing that his duty to serve the throne was greater than the Dharma of standing against injustice.

Most of us are like Bhishma. We see the wrong, we know the truth, yet we stay silent, convincing ourselves that staying focused on our path is righteousness. But such indifference is a sin as grave as his.

Many a time in life, it is not a lack of talent or intelligence that stops a person from succeeding. The real reason is that they do not perform their Karma in the right direction when it is required most. The illusion of Maya clouds their mind, whispering doubts, making them believe they are not capable, that they do not have enough resources, that success is too far away, or that others are luckier and talented. Slowly, these thoughts build walls of self-doubt inside them, blocking the beautiful path towards success and achievement. Yet, if we turn the pages of history, we find the names of those who chose to believe in themselves with true Shraddha. They performed their Karma with a full heart, without worrying about results, without getting shaken by what others said, and without surrendering to the storms of their doubts.

Many people fall into the illusion of comparing themselves with others instead of recognising their strengths and walking their path of Dharma. One of the greatest false assumptions that has captured people today is the search for shortcuts to success. Many believe that hard work is unnecessary at times, that success can come easily, and that luck matters more than effort. However, this is a false belief created by Maya, which makes people avoid the real path of perseverance and dedication.

Maya touches every person differently, taking different forms according to one's own thoughts, experiences, awareness, and the kind of guidance one has received. Yet, in its deepest nature, Maya is always the same, creating a veil over the truth. It is like a shadow; though it walks with every one of us, few ever stop to notice it. That is why in our daily lives, the presence of Maya remains so silent, almost unheard of. It quietly captures the mind, and when we try to justify or deny its existence, we unknowingly give it even more strength. To rise above Maya, it is necessary to face the truth with courage, to seek wise advice with an open heart, and to humbly accept our own inner flaws and weaknesses. Especially when doubts begin to cloud every corner of our lives, it becomes even more important to recognise Maya and break free from its quiet grip.

Maya misguides the path and misreads the heart, blinding wisdom and tearing true Dharma apart.

Many people hesitate to express their true feelings, assuming that their loved ones already know how much they care. But love and relationships also require performing Karma, an effort to express and nurture emotions. A small gesture, a kind word, or a sincere act of appreciation can bring immense joy to another person. However, Maya makes people assume that words and actions are unnecessary, leading to emotional distance. But when a person chooses to act and express their feelings without hesitation, it becomes a pure act of Karma, breaking the initial cycle of Maya.

Maya also hides itself in the form of assumptions. And many of these assumptions begin with just two simple words: 'I know!' Perhaps 'I know' has become the most repeated phrase spoken by almost every human walking on this beautiful Earth. 'I know how it works', 'I know how it feels', 'I know when to stop', 'I know how to live', 'I know this', 'I know that', 'I know what you are about to say', these small declarations keep arising, not once in a while, but almost as often as the number of breaths we take every day. There is no harm in saying 'I know'. Surely, you may know many things through your experiences and learning. But this phrase is not meant to be used so frequently unless one has truly understood, deeply experienced, and become fully aware of every dimension of that aspect. Often, saying I know too easily shuts the door to knowing more, to realising deeper truths, and to becoming aware of the mysteries that still lie hidden. At this point, it is Karma that must rise above Maya. Karma must inspire us to explore, to seek, and to grow wiser. Yet, it is the nature of Maya to hold Karma back, to cloud the eyes of curiosity, and to trap the seeker in the illusion that nothing more needs to be discovered.

Just imagine, if Goddess Parvati had said 'I know' when Lord Shankar began to reveal the mysteries of the universe, the secrets of yoga, the truth of life, the sacredness of sound, silence, breath, and awareness, what would have happened? Those ancient treasures of wisdom, which later flowed through time into our scriptures, practices, and meditations, might have remained hidden in silence.

Time carries numerous stories—some trapped in Maya and some that rose beyond it. One such story is of Bharthari, the elder brother of King Vikramaditya of Ujjain.

Though Bharthari was a wise and powerful ruler, deep within, he felt an emptiness. Despite having a kingdom, wealth, and respect, he realised these were only temporary gifts. Maya had wrapped him in the illusion of happiness through power and love. But when betrayal and sorrow struck, he saw the truth: Nothing in this world lasts forever. What use was kingship if it could not bring real peace? What value was power if it only fed more desires?

With this realisation, Bharthari left the throne and the illusions of worldly life. He handed the kingdom to Vikramaditya and chose the path of Dharma through meditation and spiritual search. He did not escape his Karma; he simply let go of the belief that he owned them. His story reminds us that karma binds only when we believe we are the doers.

Just as a computer system gets affected by a virus, in the same way, Maya acts like a virus that attacks our core operating system, our Karma. To remove this virus, we must first recognise its source, understand how it works, and see how it silently enters and operates within us. Only then can we install the antivirus of truth, through awareness, right understanding, and inner strength, to clean the system and allow our Karma to function smoothly and freely once again.

Maya builds a wall, and Karma breaks it with Dharma's call.

As time passes by, under the quiet influence of Maya, many people slowly slip into negativity and sadness. When the right time comes to perform their Karma, they choose excuses and laziness instead of action. And when that time passes, all that remains are regrets and old stories. Maya traps them in a cycle where they do nothing but sit in sorrow, blame others, point fingers, and play the victim card for their lack of success and unfulfilled actions. Instead of taking responsibility and moving forward, they stay stuck on doubts, forgetting that true freedom lies in performing Karma without delay, without affecting the desired outcome.

One of my dear friends is such a grand champion of Maya that if there were Olympic medals for self-deception, he would bring home the gold without even practising. He is firmly convinced that his Karma is on the right path, even though that train derailed long ago and is now somewhere lost in the jungle of excuses. His daily habits are a masterpiece of illusion. He spends hours gossiping about others but assures himself he is simply 'sending positive energy their way', as if judgement now comes with a blessing. He talks passionately about health and fitness, usually while munching on his third samosa, believing that discussing wellness burns as many calories as exercising. His bookshelf is a proud museum of borrowed books, untouched and gathering dust, because his Maya secretly believes wisdom will leak into his mind by osmosis.

He loves giving motivational speeches to struggling souls but somehow forgets to apply a single word of his own advice, mistaking powerful words for powerful action. He clicks hundreds of photos in temples just to showcase his 'spiritual journey' on social media, believing that online likes are a higher form of devotion than inner awareness. He proudly claims to be working on his patience yet honks furiously in traffic jams. His dream project is on permanent hold, waiting for that perfect, magical day when the stars align, the winds sing, and he finally feels 'ready', not realising that procrastination has just worn a business suit and renamed itself 'strategy'.

Yet, despite all this, his story is not to mock; it is a mirror for all of us. A funny, honest reminder that Maya thrives best where we weave little illusions for ourselves. Only by laughing at our tricks and waking up can we step onto the real path of Karma, growth, and true freedom.

In the case of my friend, assumptions have tied themselves around his Karma so tightly that he now lives in a world of his own thoughts, without even realising what he is truly doing. Maya has turned him into a happy-looking zombie—he walks, talks, and makes big plans, but when it comes to understanding the deeper truths of time, life, and existence, he remains unaware.

Sometimes, misinterpretation quietly becomes the root of false assumptions. It often begins when we read books without a full understanding, listen to influential figures without questioning, watch half-informed videos, or accept advice without deep reflection. With limited knowledge, the mind easily weaves Maya, creating wrong beliefs about our abilities, ideas of success, and the right path to achieve our goals. Slowly, these false assumptions blur the line between truth and imagination, making hesitation and self-doubt grow faster within. Over time, this confusion quietly blocks the flow of true Karma, pushing us further away from the actions we were meant to perform.

For this, as Kautilya says in Niti Shastra, every person must verify and validate knowledge, small or big, through trusted sources or guidance from the wise. True wisdom does not come easily from simply reading a few books, attending talks, watching motivational videos, or merely growing older. It comes from deep reflection, real experiences, and sincere learning over time.

At last, the sooner we identify the termites eating away at our thought process in the form of Maya, the easier it becomes to focus on our Dharma and Karma with complete Shraddha and Saburi throughout this beautiful and priceless life.

Exercise

Imagine yourself standing before the sharpest minds, sharing your insights on success, not as mere motivation, but as a practical blueprint woven with the wisdom of Karma.

Now, take a moment. Define three beliefs of Karma you hold about achieving success. These could be about hard work, destiny, persistence, talent, or luck. Write them down.

Now, critically evaluate each belief through the lens of rationality.

- Does this belief align with reality, or is it influenced by Maya (illusion), hesitation, or half-truths?
- Has it been validated by your experience, or is it simply a doubt that 'feels right'?
- Does it push you to act with conviction, or does it subtly breed self-doubt, delay, or complacency?

By examining your assumptions from a third-person perspective, you can strip away emotional biases. The goal is simple: Refine your beliefs until they serve you, not restrain you.

If a belief drives action and resilience, nurture it. If it hinders action and clouds judgement, replace it.

Key Takeaways

Maya is a false reality shaped by misconceptions, assumptions, and half-truths. It keeps people trapped in doubt, hesitation, and inaction, leading them to delay or overlook their Karma, seek shortcuts, or fear effort. Many fail not due to a lack of talent but because they let doubt, comparison, and false beliefs dictate their Karma.

5

Viveka over Assumptions

Seeking True Wisdom

मनः कल्पितमज्ञानं तत्सर्वं विवेकतः।
अविद्यायाः परं ज्ञानं यथा ज्योतिः तमः क्षयः॥

One of the most valuable lessons from the Vivekachudamani by Adi Shankaracharya (Verse 125) is that our minds often create the confusion and ignorance we experience in life. However, these illusions can be removed through wisdom and discernment (Viveka). Just as light naturally eliminates darkness, true knowledge has the power to destroy false assumptions, misunderstandings, doubts, and illusions.

Similarly, the Hitopadesha (Vidya Prakaranam, 10.3) offers a powerful metaphor to explain the difference between mere possession of knowledge and true understanding. It states that a donkey carrying sandalwood on its back only feels the weight but never experiences the fragrance. In the same way, a person who blindly assumes things or gathers information without truly experiencing its meaning remains burdened by their ignorance. They may carry knowledge, but they fail to realise its depth and significance of wisdom.

Wisdom is not just about gathering facts or believing in information; it is about understanding reality with clarity and deeper knowledge. True professional success and personal growth come when we use Viveka (discriminative intelligence) to separate truth from illusion, facts from assumptions, doubts from actions, Adharma from our Karma and wisdom from ignorance.

Lord Krishna in the Bhagavad Gita says that there is nothing as purifying in this world as Viveka (wisdom) aligned with Dharma. It is the highest virtue, the supreme cleanser of the soul, the remover of doubts, and the guiding force that leads us towards joyful life and, at last, liberation.

Chanakya Niti beautifully explains that knowledge imparts humility, which leads to worthiness. This brings wealth, wealth fosters righteousness, and righteousness leads to ultimate happiness. This is the chain reaction of true wisdom; it is not merely intellectual learning but a force that shapes our very existence.

The Greek philosopher Socrates, known for his deep search for truth, once said, 'The only true wisdom is in knowing you know nothing.' In a similar spirit, expressed in the Rigveda 4.27.1 by Sage Vamadeva, 'The Unborn supports the born, and the born one enters into the Unborn.'

Viveka is like a guiding lamp that lights up the darkness created by assumptions and Maya. It is not just information collected through the five senses; true Viveka is the wisdom that rises from within, born through self-realisation, life experiences, and understanding the deeper dimensions of existence and the self. Having Viveka is far greater than having millions of rupees. Money can buy comfort, but Viveka brings true meaning and depth to life, for there is much more to experience beyond material pleasures. Those who carry Viveka live joyfully under any circumstances, while those without it often find themselves complaining and feeling empty, no matter what they achieve. In truth, Viveka is the real wealth that makes life meaningful, turning it into an inspiring example for others. Money, success, and achievements can come through hard work or sometimes fate, but the way we choose to live our lives is decided by the presence of Viveka within us.

Either live in illusion or rise with inner clarity.

Many a time, people are unable to live happily and peacefully because they believe they lack the comforts and luxuries enjoyed by the rich. They think happiness will only arrive once they have a heavy bank balance. But the reality is different. Half the time, people chase wealth and success not because they truly need it, but because they want to prove something to others, to show the world that they are capable, to satisfy a hidden sense of ego. This subtle desire to prove oneself is nothing but a silent waste of precious energy. Such individuals need Viveka—to understand that ego is like a desert, no matter how much water you pour into it, it will never turn into an ocean. Similarly, ego can never be satisfied; it keeps demanding more and more, trapping the person in endless doubts.

On the other hand, those blessed with Viveka choose a path of Dharma. They do not waste their life proving anything to the world. They quietly stay in their zone of joy, living life as a blessing and a gift. They grow not by accumulation, but by sharing, spreading their happiness with those who have less, making their life truly rich, peaceful, and purposeful.

In today's materialistic world, many people wrongly assume that their collection of degrees, their age, or the amount of information they have gathered automatically makes them a person of wisdom. But this is not true. To truly understand the difference between information, knowledge, wisdom, and Viveka, one must sit with the truly wise, discuss with open humility, and seek deeper understanding. Only then can these elements be experienced in their real form. Otherwise, they all get mixed up in the mind, creating nothing but a wasteful resource, just like a donkey carrying sandalwood on its back, unaware of the fragrance it holds. Without true Viveka, even the greatest information becomes a weight rather than a blessing.

One of my friends has an incredible talent for making assumptions without ever using his Viveka (discerning wisdom). His ability to assume things, especially in the day-to-day, is both unimaginable and hilariously entertaining. For instance, he firmly believes that pressing the elevator button multiple times will make it arrive faster. He confidently assumes that if he says, 'I will be there in five minutes', people will actually believe him. He also thinks that talking loudly on the phone somehow strengthens the signal. His morning routine includes hitting the snooze button five times, under the impression that it means he has slept for five extra hours. He considers sending a 'Good Morning' message in a WhatsApp group as a significant social contribution. His assumptions don't stop there. He has assumed that a mosquito buzzing in his ear is specifically targeting him for some past revenge. Perhaps the funniest of all, he believes that if he pretends to be asleep when someone calls, they will think he was really asleep! With assumptions like these, life around him is never dull!

The human brain is naturally designed to recognise patterns and predict outcomes, helping us make quick decisions. But when information is incomplete, the mind instinctively fills the gaps, creating a story that feels true but may not be accurate. An assumption is nothing more than a false belief, built on a mixture of incomplete or misunderstood information. Information by itself can provide some knowledge about a subject, but it does not automatically become wisdom. Wisdom needs deeper understanding, experience, and inner clarity, something mere information alone cannot provide. If you want to confirm this, simply ask a general knowledge question or a puzzle to a ten- or twelve-year-old child. Many children, even with half or less information, will confidently answer based on their own logic. While it shows a smart use of mind, it is still a superior form of assumption, an answer created by connecting whatever little information they have, and not by full knowledge. In the same way, adults, too, sometimes make decisions or have conversations based not on complete understanding but on clever assumptions, which may not always lead to the right outcome.

Neuroscientific studies show that assumptions originate in the prefrontal cortex, the brain's decision-making centre. Faced with uncertainty, the brain defaults to familiar conclusions rather than objectively assessing new information. While assumptions help simplify life, unchecked, they distort reality and reinforce biases. Recognising this tendency allows for more conscious and accurate perception.

This is why there is a significant difference between information, knowledge, and wisdom. Information helps one become aware of something new, knowledge enables a person to overcome doubts, but wisdom goes a step further, it eliminates false assumptions—Maya—and brings true clarity about the purpose of life and success.

This is why assumptions are subjective, as they are based on personal interpretations and limited perspectives, whereas Viveka is transformative, as it changes the way a person thinks, perceives, and acts.

If you truly seek the truth, abandon illusions and let Viveka light your path.

To bring about true transformation within, one needs strong dedication and commitment. A determined person can achieve this growth with ease, but someone filled with hesitation will continue to struggle. Their duality of thought keeps them stuck, making them swing between overthinking and analysis paralysis. Instead of moving forward, they remain trapped in endless mental debates, never reaching a decisive conclusion towards Viveka.

Thus, the key to success lies in breaking free from the cycle of assumptions and striving for true wisdom through conscious effort and clarity about Dharma.

Wisdom is the key to a meaningful, flawless life. One free from unnecessary sorrows, repentance, and worries. It is a life full of vitality, one that transcends ego, greed, lust, illusions, and false perceptions and hallucinations. Everyone, knowingly or unknowingly, seeks this perfection throughout life, yet few realise where to find it.

A similar example can be seen in Ravana's story. He assumed that his immense power, numerous boons, and the golden kingdom of Lanka made him invincible. Believing himself to be undefeatable, he thought he had the right to do whatever he wished, even if it meant kidnapping another man's wife. Ravana was a great scholar, a master of warfare, music, astrology, and Ayurveda. Yet despite all his knowledge, he lacked wisdom in the most important aspects of life—humanity, ethics, and morality.

Both Karna and Ravana were highly capable individuals, yet their assumptions led them astray. Karna believed he had to prove his worth to society in the wrong way, and Ravana believed his strength made him above all laws of righteousness.

If they had focused on seeking wisdom instead of holding onto their false beliefs, their stories could have taken a completely different turn.

However, it is our primary responsibility to seek wisdom from the most authentic and reliable sources. True wisdom is not something we can assume or fabricate; it must be discovered through deep exploration and experience. In this journey, ancient Hindu scriptures serve as invaluable guides. The Vedas, Puranas, Bhagavad Gita, Ramayana, Mahabharata, Upanishads, and the teachings of great spiritual gurus provide profound insights into the nature of truth and Dharma. These sacred texts have been tested over centuries and offer a path to clarity and enlightenment.

However, one must be extremely careful when distinguishing true Viveka from misleading or distorted interpretations. In today's world, where falsehoods often come in more attractive and persuasive packaging than the original, it is easy to be deceived. Many sources claim to offer wisdom but are merely diluted or altered versions, designed to appeal to people's emotions rather than guide them towards the ultimate truth.

Another important responsibility is to accept wisdom in its purest form, without modifying it to fit personal preferences or desires. The truth remains unchanged, whether one agrees with it or not. If a person tries to mould wisdom according to their convenience, they move away from reality and trap themselves in illusion. By accepting wisdom without hesitation, one closes the doors to assumptions, which otherwise can lead to confusion, doubts, poor decisions, and even self-destruction.

Hesitation often gives rise to assumptions. When a person lacks the courage to face reality or fears the journey ahead, they begin relying on their imagination to create assumptions. Instead of seeking clarity, they choose to fill the gaps with guesses and personal interpretations, which may not be accurate. This is why hesitation is one of the root causes of false beliefs, as it prevents people from seeing things as they truly are and instead leads them to seek comfort in their imagined versions of reality.

As we grow, our thoughts and personalities develop with traits, flaws, and hesitation. We gain knowledge through our senses, collecting information from the external world. However, intelligence built upon borrowed knowledge is not wisdom. Wisdom is an internal understanding derived from lived experiences. It cannot be attained through mere reading, hearing, or assumptions; it comes only through direct realisation.

For instance, knowing that a hot pan can burn your hand is different from actually touching it and feeling the pain of heat. The real experience of heat and pain is what leads to true wisdom in this subject matter.

Similarly, a person who wins a gold medal in swimming may know all the theories of swimming, but unless they have truly swum in water, they cannot understand the real touch and feel of it. Experience makes a person truly wise, beyond any illusions or false assumptions.

That is why life is all about experiencing. Nobody can hold onto a single moment or keep anything permanently. Our experiences depend on our actions and their consequences, the reactions of people, and the natural laws of life.

Similarly, many people tend to assume their worth based on their perceived creativity, intelligence, or talent. They believe that these qualities alone define them, without questioning whether their self-perception aligns with reality. However, creativity, talent, and intelligence are often subjective and do not always guarantee success or recognition. Assumptions about one's abilities can be misleading, as they are sometimes exaggerated and/or may not hold true over time. Thus, it is important to constantly test and refine one's skills through real-world experiences rather than solely relying on assumptions.

An inspiring story from the Markandeya Purana tells us about King Harishchandra, a ruler known for his unwavering commitment to truth and righteousness. One day, the great sage Vishwamitra decided to test his devotion to dharma and demanded everything from him. Harishchandra did not assume that the gods had abandoned him or question in hesitation why he was being put through such hardships. Instead, he chose the path of Viveka and remained firm in his belief that Satya (truth) and Dharma (righteousness) must never be compromised.

Without hesitation, he gave away his entire kingdom and wealth, accepting the challenges that came his way. He even took up work as a cremation ground keeper, sold his wife, and endured suffering, but never wavered from his principles. Despite all the difficulties, he remained true to his word. In the end, the sage, pleased with his dedication and wisdom, restored his kingdom and honoured him. His story became an eternal symbol of truth and wisdom, reminding people that real success is not about material wealth but about standing by one's values even in the face of adversity.

On the other hand, Duryodhana's story in the Mahabharata teaches the opposite lesson. He assumed that victory in the Kurukshetra war was assured simply because he had a larger army. With eleven Akshauhini sena compared to the Pandavas' seven Akshauhini sena, he was confident that sheer numbers would guarantee his success. Moreover, he had some of the greatest warriors on his side—Bhishma, Drona, Karna, Ashwatthama, Kripacharya, Shalya, Bhurisravas, Bhagadatta,

Vrishasena, and Kritavarma—all of whom had never been defeated in battle.

However, Duryodhana failed to understand a deeper truth: Victory does not belong to power alone, but to righteousness. He overlooked the fact that quality matters more than quantity and that divine justice always favours those who stand for truth and virtue. The Pandavas, though fewer in number, fought with wisdom, unity, and righteousness, which ultimately led them to victory.

Like Duryodhana, the Mughals and Adilshahis believed in the power of numbers. They controlled vast empires, had massive armies, and unlimited resources. In comparison, Chatrapati Shivaji Maharaj started as a young warrior with a small army, limited resources, and surrounded by enemies.

However, unlike Duryodhana, Chatrapati Shivaji Maharaj understood that true power lies in Dharma, Viveka, Satya, and Kartavya, along with the will of the people and divine blessings. He had no hesitation towards his goal to create Hindavi Swaraj. Just as Lord Krishna guided the Pandavas, Saint Eknath, Saint Tukaram, Swami Samarth, and Samarth Ramdas supported Chatrapati Shivaji Maharaj, blessing him with wisdom, strength, and spiritual guidance. Goddess Bhavani herself blessed Chatrapati Shivaji with a sword, symbolising that his fight was for Dharma and Swaraj, not just personal ambition.

Throughout history and sacred scriptures, the lesson remains unchanged: Viveka (wisdom) triumphs over assumptions, and righteousness (Dharma) prevails over blind arrogance. Viveka is the key to success in both personal and professional life. It helps us see beyond illusions and hesitation, act with clarity, and make decisions that align with truth and justice.

Remember, success belongs not to those who assume but to those who choose wisdom.

Exercise

Imagine that you have just discovered the exact date of your death, exactly one year from today. You now have only 365 days left to achieve success in your profession, whether it's in business, a job, or any other pursuit.

Now, take a pen and paper and write down your action plan for these final 365 days to achieve the desired success. Focus on what steps you need to take immediately to make the most of your time.

Once you complete this exercise, you will notice something remarkable—your plan is based entirely on your wisdom, clarity, and decisive action, with no room for any assumptions, vague expectations, or hesitation. You will no longer rely on thoughts like:

- 'Maybe things will work out on their own.'
- 'Someone might help me.'
- 'I assume the situation will change in my favour.'

Instead, every action will be intentional and based on reality. When you replace hesitation with priority, assumptions automatically disappear, leaving behind pure wisdom and clarity.

This exercise reveals a powerful truth: Success is never achieved through assumptions, but through focused, well-planned, and decisive actions. When you act as if time is limited, you automatically operate with wisdom, taking only the most essential and impactful steps. Now, ask yourself, why wait for urgency to develop this mindset? Why not eliminate assumptions and apply wisdom in your life today?

Key Takeaways

Viveka is the ability to perceive reality without illusions or false assumptions. It requires self-reflection, patience, and discernment, while assumptions are mere hesitation and shortcuts that lead to confusion and poor decisions. Many people rely on assumptions due to fear or hesitation, which limits their growth and traps them in self-doubt. In contrast, wisdom, gained through knowledge and experience, provides clarity, direction, and confidence. True success comes not from intelligence or power alone but from applying wisdom in life's challenges. Choosing wisdom over assumption and hesitation leads to truth, righteousness, and a purposeful life.

6

Dharma and Kartavya

Balancing Duty without Compromise

श्रेयान्स्वधर्मो विगुणः परधर्मात्स्वनुष्ठितात्।
स्वधर्मे निधनं श्रेयः परधर्मो भयावहः॥

One of the most valuable lessons from the Mahabharata (3.35), this shloka teaches that one must fulfil their duties and responsibilities sincerely. It warns against abandoning one's designated duty (Kartavya) for something that is not meant for them, as doing so can lead to confusion and failure.

Dharma is the deeper, universal principle that holds life together. Dharma is not just about obeying rules; it is about doing what is truly right, based on the situation, time, nature, and the voice of our inner conscience. Dharma touches every corner of life—how we think, how we speak, how we act, and how we connect with others, with nature, and with ourselves. It is wide like the sky. It includes moral duties, spiritual truths, kindness, justice, and the art of living in a way that uplifts both oneself and the world around.

Kartavya, on the other hand, is more personal and practical. Kartavya simply means our duty, what we must do in a particular role, situation, or relationship. It is the action side of Dharma. While Dharma shows the eternal truth, Kartavya portrays how we can bring that truth into our daily lives.

Dharma is the foundation, and Kartavya is the action that rises from it.

Let's make a list of the top 100 successful achievers in the world out of billions of people. We will notice one thing in common is that in one or the other means, these people have understood and accepted their Dharma towards their goals and ambitions. They are putting their Kartavya with devoted consistency. This is the simplest secret, and this is the only difference between the world and these achievers.

Most people in the world are living without even realising their true Dharma. Especially when it comes to their own Kartavya, their duty towards themselves, their faith in humanity and values, their dedication towards their efforts, their trust in universal justice, and their overall approach towards this beautiful life. Without this awareness, many continue to live in doubt, chasing temporary goals but missing the deeper meaning and true purpose of their journey. Recognising one's Dharma brings clarity, strength, and a sense of deep connection to life itself.

Nobody in this world likes to compromise on their dreams, ambitions, and goals. Every person wishes to grow, succeed, and achieve something meaningful in life. Yet, we often see many people settling for less, letting go of their ambitions, and compromising on things that once mattered deeply to them.

But why do people compromise?

People compromise not because they lack dreams and ambitions, but because they remain stuck in a constant battle within their minds. They hesitate to make that extra effort, fearing the unknown, unsure whether their hard work will bear the desired outcome. The fear of failure grips them so tightly that they choose safety above growth and comfort over courage. Either laziness stops them from working sincerely, or their constant search for shortcuts diverts them from the real path. Some get lost in comfort and endless entertainment, while others remain stuck in the never-ending see-saw of analysis paralysis. In all cases, precious time slips away, and without realising, they allow distractions to steal their dreams and delay their own growth.

That's why performing one's Kartavya according to Dharma is the key to rising above all and living life to the fullest with no regrets and no chance of failure.

If we look closely, there are two types of compromises in life. The first one happens when circumstances are beyond our control. Sometimes, due to unavoidable situations, we must adjust, let go, or change our path. This kind of compromise is natural and necessary. It helps us accept life's realities and move forward with performing the required Kartavya.

However, the second type of compromise is self-created, which occurs because of hesitation, fear, and self-doubt. It is when a person steps back, not because of an external force, but because they are afraid to take a step forward. They choose hesitation over courage and doubts over their own abilities. Sadly, this kind of compromise is more common, and people do it without even realising how much they are losing.

A person with great ideas may stay silent in a meeting because they fear being judged. A young woman who dreams of being an artist may never show her paintings because she worries that others won't appreciate them. A student with potential may not apply for a prestigious college because they think they are not good enough. These are not compromises forced by life, they are decisions made under hesitation. And in the long run, doubts costs more than failure ever will.

Many people think that compromise is a noble act, a sign of humility and goodness. Society often praises those who give up their desires for others. But the truth is, such compromise hides unfulfilled potential, lost opportunities, and great regrets. It is not always a virtue; sometimes, it is just a mask that covers a life that could have been much more.

If one must compromise, let it be for growth, wisdom, and peace, not out of fear, hesitation, or self-doubt. In the end, people do not regret their failures as much as they regret the efforts they never tried to initiate. So, the next time you hesitate, ask yourself: Am I compromising because I have no choice or because I am afraid to try?

One of my friends has completely misinterpreted the idea of Kartavya, shaping it in ways that are both amusing and questionable. For him, watching YouTube tutorials instead of actually learning is his Kartavya towards being knowledgeable. Forwarding WhatsApp festival wishes is his Kartavya towards world unity and collective celebration. Giving unsolicited advice in random discussions is his Kartavya as the self-proclaimed wise person of the group. He believes that laughing at a joke even when he doesn't understand it is his Kartavya to maintain social harmony. Ignoring traffic rules but blaming the system is, in his mind, his Kartavya as a true citizen. Checking his phone fifty times a day is his Kartavya to stay updated on world affairs.

His sense of duty extends to taking credit for team efforts, which he considers his Kartavya as an inspiring leader.

Pretending to listen while scrolling through his phone is his version of Kartavya in the name of multitasking. Leaving one last bite of food on his plate is, to him, an act of dieting, and starting a new habit every Monday only to quit by Wednesday is his Kartavya towards self-improvement.

However, the truth is, these are not just his assumptions, many people around us believe they are fulfilling their Kartavya in similar ways, thinking they are balancing both Karma and Dharma simultaneously. But the real question remains: Is it truly happening the way it should?

My guru once shared a beautiful story.

> A great Guru lived in a dense jungle with his five disciples. Their life was extremely simple, there was little food, harsh weather, dry soil, fallen trees, and snakes all around. One day, a disciple complained, 'Guruji, you have great powers. Why don't you turn this jungle into a paradise?'
>
> The Guru smiled and replied, 'Accept things as they are. Do not fall into the trap of expecting comfort and pleasure and compromising with your wisdom of acceptance. Instead, experience life as it comes, with full awareness.'
>
> The very next day, a king came to the jungle for hunting. He saw the Guru and recognised his greatness. Out of respect, he invited the Guru and his disciples to stay in his palace for a few days. The Guru agreed, and they all went to the palace.
>
> The king provided them with luxurious food, comfortable beds, and grand entertainment, including mesmerising dance performances by the finest dancers.
>
> The Guru enjoyed everything. He ate heartily, rested on soft cushions, and watched the performances with joy.

> One disciple, feeling confused and embarrassed, asked, 'Guruji, how can you enjoy all this? You always teach us to live with what life offers. But now, you are enjoying luxury. Have you forgotten your teachings?'
>
> The Guru smiled and said, 'I told you to experience life as it is fully without attachment. Yesterday, we had nothing, yet we accepted it with joy. Today, we have abundance, and we should accept it with the same joy but without getting attached to it and compromising with our motive. If we become attached, our mind will always crave such pleasures, and we shall never compromise with our true purpose.'

In today's fast-moving world, people often overlook their Dharma and Kartavya. Dharma is the set of actions required as per one's role and responsibility, while Kartavya is something that must be done without compromise. Both are deeply connected, Kartavya should always be performed with Dharma at its core, ensuring that our actions remain just, fair, and meaningful.

Kartavya is not just a word; it is a lifelong commitment. It applies to every stage of life, from childhood to old age. A child's Kartavya is to study well, develop good habits, and learn the art of living through their parents' *Sanskara* (values and teachings). A child who ignores this Kartavya may struggle later in life, lacking discipline and direction. Similarly, a young man's Kartavya is to shape his life in a way that benefits both his family and society. He must focus on growth, hard work, and ethical conduct. A young man who chases shortcuts and ignores responsibilities often ends up in confusion, analysis paralysis and regret. A householder's Kartavya is to perform all duties towards family, work, and society while keeping Dharma in the centre. This means being fair, just, and honest in all dealings, whether in business, job, or family matters. A person who compromises their integrity for personal gain loses the essence of both Dharma and Kartavya.

Lastly, an elder's Kartavya is to guide the next generation using their life's wisdom and the teachings of scriptures. Their experiences serve as a lighthouse for the younger generation, helping them avoid mistakes and walk on the right path. But if elders stay silent due to hesitation, their knowledge remains unshared, and the younger generation loses valuable guidance.

Sadly, doubt makes people leave their Kartavya half-done. They fail to act when needed, making excuses or fearing judgement.

I had a friend, a man of immense talent in film-making, whose understanding of screenplay was remarkable, and his acting skills were extraordinary. He had everything needed to create magic on screen, yet he walked away from the industry. Not because he lacked potential, but because he had plenty of excuses, no high-quality cameras, no crew members, no financial backing, no technical support, etc.

Were these real obstacles or just his hesitation wrapped in excuses? Instead of finding ways around the hurdles and using whatever he had to create something, even if it was raw but powerful enough to grab the attention of great film-makers, he chose inaction. He could have started small, made films with whatever was available, but he waited for perfect conditions that never arrived.

Years later, when he saw young creators making films with just mobile phones, editing on simple apps, and gaining recognition, he felt lost. By then, he was forty-eight, with nothing but regret in his heart—of abandoning his dreams, his passion, his very purpose. Not because he wasn't capable, but because he hesitated to take that first step. He turned away from his Kartavya, his duty to his potential. He left behind his Dharma, the path he was meant to walk. In doing so, he lost not just a career, but a part of himself.

Imagine if Chhatrapati Shivaji Maharaj had hesitated to build Swaraj, fearing the mighty Mughal Empire. Think about what if Mahatma Gandhi had stayed back in South Africa, focusing on his successful legal career instead of answering his Kartavya towards the nation? Would India have ever witnessed the power of non-violence and truth?

What if Lord Ram had chosen rebellion over duty, refusing exile and not fighting for righteousness? His story would not have been remembered as the ideal of Dharma and Kartavya, and he would not be worshipped as Maryada Purushottam.

And what if Lord Krishna, standing in the battlefield of Kurukshetra, had hesitated to share his wisdom with Arjun? What if he had thought, *Let Arjun decide on his own. Why should I interfere?* The Bhagavad Gita, which today serves as a guiding light for millions, would never have been spoken, and Arjun might have walked away from his destiny out of confusion and duality.

Now, ask yourself if history would have been the same if these great souls had hesitated? Or would they have been forgotten in time, just like the countless others who allowed fear and doubt to rule their decisions?

Every day, billions of people stand at the crossroads of choice, whether to follow their Dharma and Kartavya or to step back out of doubts and compromise. Those who choose fear over action fade away into time, leaving behind nothing but regrets. But those who rise above their doubts and take responsibility carve their names in history, shaping their destiny and inspiring generations to come.

So, when life presents you with a difficult choice, remember these great souls. You may not be leading an empire, fighting for a nation, or delivering divine wisdom, but in your own way, your actions matter. Your Dharma and Kartavya define who you are and what you leave behind.

Will you rise and act, or will you hesitate and fade into time? The choice is yours.

The Bhagavata Purana (Canto 6) gives us one of the greatest examples of Kartavya in line with Dharma. The story of Sage Dadhichi, a sage known for his deep penance and selflessness. When the gods were losing the battle against the powerful demons, they needed a weapon strong enough to defeat their enemies. But such a weapon could only be made from the bones of a pure and noble sage. Without a moment's hesitation, Rishi Dadhichi willingly sacrificed his own life, allowing his bones to be used to create the Vajrayudha (thunderbolt weapon) for Lord Indra. This weapon later became the key to defeating the demon Vritra and restoring balance in the universe.

A similar lesson is found in the Shibi Jataka, where King Shibi became the symbol of unwavering duty and righteousness. One day, a dove, terrified and exhausted, flew into his court and sought refuge. A hawk, chasing the dove, appeared before the king and demanded his rightful meal. Unknown to Shibi, this was a divine test, as the hawk was Lord Indra in disguise. The Kartavya of a king is to protect the weak, and Shibi did not waver. Instead of handing over the dove, he offered his flesh as a substitute. To prove his sincerity, he placed his own body on a scale, cutting his flesh to match the dove's weight. Pleased with his unshakable righteousness, the gods revealed their true forms and blessed him, declaring that he was a king worthy of divine respect.

Therefore, life becomes truly meaningful when we learn to balance Dharma and Kartavya without compromise. It is this balance that brings inner greatness, a burden-free life, and opens doors to prosperity and growth. Many people think that following Dharma and fulfilling Kartavya requires extraordinary abilities, but the truth is, it needs nothing more than a strong will and sincere commitment. It is not some complex philosophy or rocket science. It simply requires a willingness to act and a deep sense of responsibility.

Following Dharma and performing Kartavya does not guarantee wealth or fame, but it ensures something far more important—a life well-lived, free from guilt, filled with self-respect, and lived with a full heart. In the end, what matters is not how much we earn, but how we live, what we stand for, and the respect we hold in our own eyes.

Exercise

Imagine you are given a superpower—the ability to become invisible whenever you want.

Now, take a moment. Think deeply and honestly. If you had this power, how would you use it? Take out your notebook, the one you have kept for this book's self-reflection exercises and write your answer with complete sincerity and truth.

Would you:

- Use your invisibility sneaking into places to fulfil lust, greed, or personal gain?

or

- Use it for a noble purpose to serve society, protect the weak, fight injustice, or bring positive change?

Now, reflect on your answer. If your answer leans towards the first option, you have already compromised on Dharma and Kartavya. You have allowed temptation and personal interests to overshadow your duty. However, if your answer aligns with the second option, it means you have the strength to stand by Dharma and Kartavya without hesitation or compromise. You are someone who values responsibility over self-indulgence, and for that, you deserve self-respect and appreciation.

Remember, when it comes to writing down an answer, most people, including you, instinctively choose the second option. As it is easy to pick this answer on paper, but in real-life situations, do your actions reflect the same choice?

Key Takeaways

Life is about choices, whether to compromise or to stand firm in Dharma and Kartavya. Many people give up on their dreams, not because of circumstances, but due to hesitation, fear, and self-doubt. Dharma (righteous duty) and Kartavya (responsibility) go hand in hand. The balance of Dharma and Kartavya is not rocket science; it requires a strong will and sincere commitment. It does not guarantee wealth or power, but it ensures a life of self-respect, fulfilment, and no regrets. In the end, true success is not measured by what we earn, but by how we live, the values we uphold, and the legacy we leave behind.

7

Asha and Dhairya

Hope Rooted in Patience

नाहं मन्ये सुवेदेति नो न वेदेति वेद च।
यो नस्तद्वेद तद्वेद नो न वेदेति वेद च॥

One of the most profound verses from the Kena Upanishad (2.2) reveals a gentle yet powerful truth: 'I do not think I know It well, and yet I do not think that I do not know It. He among us who knows It as "not known"—he knows It; and he who thinks he knows It—he does not know It.'

This paradox offers quiet hope—urging the seeker to continue with faithful effort and silent patience. True knowledge is not in claiming certainty, but in humbly accepting the unknown and trusting that inner clarity will unfold in time.

Hope is the unseen root that anchors the tree of destiny, holding it firm against the storms of doubt. Patience is the silent strength of the soul, where time bows to the one who waits with wisdom.

Hope is the positive energy that keeps the heart alive. It is the belief that something good can happen, that better days are possible, and that efforts are meaningful. Hope gives strength to dreams. It keeps the flame burning even in the darkest nights. Without hope, a person feels empty and defeated from within. Hope is the spark that makes us wish, imagine, and move towards a better future.

Patience, on the other hand, is the calmness and strength to wait for that better future without frustration or doubt. It is the ability to stay steady, continue efforts with faith, and trust in the Dharma. Patience is what holds a person strong when results are delayed, when challenges are heavy, or when the path becomes unclear. It protects hope from dying under the weight of waiting.

Today, if you ask someone to have patience, they may look at you as if you are speaking a forgotten language from another world. In an age where everything moves faster than we can even imagine, patience is often misunderstood. It is no longer considered a strength; instead, many treat it as something old-fashioned, something only weak or helpless people must accept. But the truth is, patience is not about helpless waiting; it is about powerful trusting. It is the quiet strength that holds dreams steady when the world rushes by without thinking. Those who truly understand patience know that real growth, real success, and real peace come only to those who are willing to walk steadily, even when everything around them runs in haste and doubt.

Life today is all about shortcuts. Need information? Ask ChatGPT, Feeling hungry? Open Zomato or Swiggy. Shopping no longer requires stepping out. Even weddings, once celebrated with months of preparation and family gatherings, are now happening online. The world has become a place where people have lost the habit of waiting. If something takes time, frustration takes over. Everyone wants everything instantly, as if patience is a burden rather than a virtue.

However, if you look at the lives of those who have built something meaningful, you will see a different story. Dashrath Manjhi, a poor labourer from the village of Gehlaur in Bihar, proved that patience, determination, and hope can achieve the impossible. His wife, Falguni Devi, was injured while crossing a treacherous mountain to bring him food. With no immediate medical help available, she lost her life. Heartbroken but determined, Manjhi resolved to carve a path through the mountain so that no one else would suffer the same fate. Armed with only a hammer and chisel, he worked tirelessly for twenty-two years (1960–1982), breaking through the massive rock, single-handedly creating a 110-meter-long road. His efforts reduced the distance between his village and the nearest town from 55 km to just 15 km, giving people easier access to hospitals, schools, and markets. Ridiculed at first, he never gave up. Today, he is remembered as the Mountain Man, an extraordinary example of how Dhairya (patience), Asha (hope), and unwavering commitment can turn the impossible into reality.

The only thing that becomes a hurdle in maintaining hope and patience is the hesitation to even think about it. People often doubt their ability to maintain hope and hesitate to follow the Dharma. Their inner fears, duality, and analysis paralysis lead them to make U-turns. It is like a farmer who keeps changing his crops again and again, simply because he has no patience and loses hope when he doesn't see quick results. Instead of nurturing what he has sown, he gives up too early, never allowing anything to grow fully.

Hope makes one race, but patience grants peace beyond needless struggle.

That's why we must learn from King Muchukunda, whose story teaches that patience and faith in divine timing always bring rewards, which is mentioned in the Bhagavata Purana (Canto 10).

He was a righteous king who fought tirelessly for the gods against the asuras (demons) for many years. When the gods finally won, they realised that Muchukunda had sacrificed his entire life for them without rest. Unable to return his lost time, they granted him a boon. He chose eternal sleep, waiting for the right moment to awaken with noble purpose. Centuries later, when Lord Krishna was being chased by the undefeated demon Kalayavana, he entered Muchukunda's cave. As soon as the demon disturbed his sleep, Muchukunda's mere gaze burned him to ashes, fulfilling the divine plan. After this, Muchukunda realised his higher purpose and renounced worldly pleasures for spiritual self-realisation. Though he waited for centuries, when the moment arrived, his role in the grand scheme of Dharma was fulfilled.

Similarly, Shabari's story is a remarkable example of unwavering Dhairya and Asha. She spent years waiting with complete faith that one day Lord Ram would visit her ashram. Despite her long wait, she never lost hope, and when the moment finally arrived, her devotion was rewarded, proving that true faith and patience always bear sweet fruit.

A striking contrast between hope and patience versus impatience and hopelessness is observed in the Mahabharata. Yudhishthira embodies patience and perseverance, enduring exile with dignity, trusting that Dharma would ultimately prevail. On the other hand, Duryodhana symbolises impatience and despair. His inability to wait, his arrogance, and his reckless rush into war without wisdom led to the destruction of his family and kingdom. These two characters remind us that while patience builds and sustains, impatience destroys everything in its path.

Krishna's unwavering patience towards Shishupala reflects the depth of his promise to Shishupala's mother, Shrutashrava. With calm resolve, he bore a hundred insults, holding on to hope and never allowing doubt to shake his word. It was not silence, but strength—proof that true power lies in honouring one's vow, even when tested by provocation.

Now, imagine if Shabari had doubted waiting for so long simply because Lord Ram never gave her a specific time or date for his arrival. Despite having no assurance of when he would come, she waited with unwavering hope. If she had been impatient, she might have abandoned her devotion and missed the divine moment to meet Lord Ram.

Doubt does not just delay action; it quietly breeds impatience. It pushes people to act without clarity, without deep thought, rushing from one thing to another. It traps them in a restless state where they refuse to believe in anything that cannot be seen, touched, or scientifically proven. Sadly, the very education that was meant to free their minds sometimes becomes a burden on their wisdom, closing the door to trust in the unseen forces that silently shape life. True growth demands not just sharp thinking but also a humble faith in what the eyes cannot always see.

In this restless state, they lose both hope and patience, believing that everything is within their control. But they forget the simplest, most profound law of nature—everything has its time. No matter how much we wish, rain will not fall before monsoon, the summer sun will not blaze before its season, and a fruit will not ripen before its due time. Life unfolds at its own pace, and true success requires effort, direction, and above all, Asha and Dhairya.

The reality of life is: Not everyone achieves grand success. Some attain massive achievements, while others find moderate success. Yet, the endless race to prove oneself to society often leads people into darkness, burdened with stress, sorrow, and painful experiences. True wisdom lies in accepting our individuality and embracing our Dharma. This acceptance liberates us from unnecessary pressure and emotional struggles, helping us to create own universe, shaped by our working style and natural abilities.

Success and failure are just outcomes. Our true role is to keep performing, to keep putting in efforts, and to keep progressing on the path we are meant to walk. This is the very lesson Lord Krishna imparted to Arjun when he hesitated to fight in the great war of Kurukshetra. Lord Krishna reminded him that his duty was to act, without attachment to results, and to perform his role sincerely, without fear or doubt or hesitation. This wisdom is the key to real success. One that is based on self-discovery, perseverance, and unwavering hope in our potential.

Success patiently waits within us to be discovered; it does not arrive at the mere calling of hope.

One of my friends is so impatient that he has never truly come across the concept of Dhairya and has no real understanding of Asha in its true sense. While he does have Shraddha, it is completely misguided, placed in things that serve no real purpose. He believes in wearing a lucky shirt before a job interview but does not prepare well, expecting divine intervention to guarantee success. He visits temples to pray for patience but immediately loses his temper if someone cuts in line. At the same time, he rushes to take *prasad* first, believing it will bring him more blessings, while pushing others aside in the line. His impatience extends to watching motivational videos by constantly skipping through the timeline, expecting life to change instantly. He complains that prayers are ineffective but keeps switching deities every month, thinking a different one might bring faster results. He seeks advice from mentors but only in search of shortcuts, refusing to invest in long-term effort. He claims to believe in karma but expects instant rewards for every small, good deed, failing to understand that real karma unfolds over time.

Such a distorted sense of Dhairya has no meaning, and such misplaced Asha leads nowhere but deeper into the illusions of Maya and self-created hallucinations. With these self-made concepts, no one can ever reach the unknown truth or attain real progress in life.

To grasp the essence of Asha and Dhairya, one must seek guidance from the wise. Those who have lived these virtues, not just learnt about them. But in today's fast-moving world, everyone believes they know everything. They mistake information for knowledge, and knowledge for wisdom, forgetting that there is a vast difference between the three.

Another essential lesson to learn is that whenever we feel hesitant, confused, or uncertain about our duties or the outcomes of our actions, we must seek guidance from the wise. Wisdom is not just about individual learning and experiencing but also about knowing Dharma, realising when to ask for advice and direction from whom.

Many people hesitate to consult those with greater wisdom, fearing that it will hurt their ego or make them appear less competent. However, the truth is that seeking wise counsel is a sign of strength, not weakness. Consulting those with experience and knowledge is the key to growth and progress.

Just as a river does not resist merging with the ocean to become vast, a person must not resist learning from the wise to grow in life.

Ignorance lives in 'I know', and true growth begins with 'let's ask'.

The greatest minds in history have sought knowledge from those before them. Even Lord Krishna, despite being the Supreme Consciousness, sought guidance from Guru Sandipani during his early years. Lord Ram, the Maryada Purushottam, learnt under Guru Vashishtha. Seeking wisdom is a natural step in the journey towards greatness.

Information fills the mind, knowledge sharpens it, but wisdom awakens the soul and reminds us of our Dharma. Let us always remember this.

A little-known man from Assam, Jadav Payeng, single-handedly transformed a barren land into a lush forest over thirty years. When he started planting trees in 1979, people mocked him. But with Asha in his vision and Dhairya to persist through decades, he created what is now called the Molai Forest, a 1,300-acre oasis that shelters elephants, tigers, and thousands of species.

Bruce Lee once said that the human mind follows only the instructions a person gives it through their thoughts. It does not operate beyond what is considered or believed. The mind shapes not just the thought process but also the body language and actions that follow. When a person thinks positively and with clarity, their body and actions align with that confidence. On the other hand, doubts alter the way the body responds. A hesitant person unknowingly reflects uncertainty in their posture, expressions, and movements.

Hesitation is not just a fleeting moment of doubt; it is a silent force that seeps into the very foundation of one's decisions, making them uncertain, impatient, and ultimately inactive. Every time a person hesitates, they unknowingly strengthen a cycle of self-doubt that holds them back from opportunities, growth, and progress. It also forces people to question their own Asha, weakening their power of Dhairya.

Research on growth mindset by Dr Carol Dweck (1988) emphasises that believing in one's ability to improve fuels motivation and persistence. Those who hesitate often fall into a fixed mindset, assuming that failure is a reflection of their limitations rather than a learning opportunity.

On the other hand, individuals who train their minds to think with conviction and act with certainty create a self-sustaining loop of confidence. They move forward not because they are fearless, but because of their hope in their ability to navigate life challenges. The ancient wisdom of Asha and Dhairya plays a crucial role. Aasha is the unwavering belief in one's path, while Dhairya is the patience to walk it, even when results are not immediate or favourable. Without Aasha, one lacks the hope to take the first step. Without Dhairya, they give up too soon, never allowing their efforts to bear fruit.

Life is not about waiting for perfect conditions or absolute certainty; it is about training the mind to trust itself, stand firm, and take action despite the unknown. The hesitation that once felt like a safety net is, in truth, the very thing that keeps a person from ever flying. The path forward is shaped not by overthinking but by the courage to move with belief, embracing the journey with Asha and Dhairya as guiding forces of Dharma.

Exercise

To test the levels of Asha and Dhairya you contain within, try a simple experiment. Meet five people with whom you do not have regular interaction but who still know you. Introduce yourself, speak about your potential, and share your aspirations and dreams.

If you find yourself feeling hesitant, awkward, or unsure while expressing your potential and dreams, then it is a sign that doubt has taken hold of you. This hesitation is not just about speaking; it also reflects a deeper self-doubt and a lack of hope in your abilities. It means you are yet to develop complete hope in yourself, the belief that you are capable, worthy, and meant to achieve something meaningful.

On the other hand, if you can express yourself with clarity and confidence, it shows that you have passed the test of Shraddha. Now, the next step is to walk forward with Dhairya, the patience to sustain your efforts until the small or big opportunities turn into success. Just like every seed takes time to grow into a strong tree, your belief in yourself must be nurtured with patience, improvement, growth and steady action.

Key Takeaways

Asha and Dhairya are not just familiar words; they are deep principles that must be lived to bring real growth. Asha is the hope that fuels belief in oneself, while Dhairya is the patience to wait for the right moment. Together, they can turn the ordinary into extraordinary. But doubts block their power. It creates impatience and inaction. To move ahead and realise one's full potential, one must overcome hesitation.

8
Klesha over Swadhyaya
From Afflictions to Self-Reflection

अविद्यास्मितारागद्वेषाभिनिवेशाः क्लेशाः॥
स्वाध्यायादिष्टदेवता संप्रयोगः॥

One of the most valuable lessons from Patanjali Yoga Sutras, this shloka beautifully explains that these afflictions cloud the mind and hinder spiritual progress. To overcome them, one must cultivate awareness, detachment, and wisdom. Moreover, through Swadhyaya (self-study and recitation of scriptures), one attains connection with their chosen deity or higher consciousness. Swadhyaya is not just about reading scriptures but deeply contemplating their meaning, reflecting on one's thoughts, and understanding one's mind. It leads to self-purification and inner wisdom.

स्वाध्यायप्रवचनाभ्यां न प्रमदितव्यम्।

The verse from the Taittiriya Upanishad (1.9.1) gently reveals that Swadhyaya, or self-study, is the sacred path to inner clarity. It clears the fog of doubt and steadies the wandering mind with a sense of direction. The scriptures, like quiet lamps glowing in the dark, do not merely instruct; they guide us inwards, towards the quiet core where true wisdom awakens.

Why Should One Perform Swadhyaya?

When we buy a new mobile phone, it comes with a user manual explaining how to use it efficiently. A company provides a policy framework to guide employees on how to work systematically. Similarly, the Bhagavad Gita offers a profound framework for human life, guiding us on how to live a peaceful and prosperous life. In the same manner, every individual must study themselves to understand their full potential, strengths, weaknesses, flaws and Dharma. This process is called Swadhyaya, where 'Swa' means self and 'Adhyaya' means study, making it a deep self-exploration.

Most people believe they know themselves well and possess full control over their bodies and minds. But let's question this assumption. Can anyone control their digestive system? Can they stop or start their urinary process at will? If people truly controlled their thoughts, why do negative thoughts arise? Who decides them? Is it the person or is the mind playing tricks? Do people consciously breathe, or does it happen on its own? Do they grow or shed their hair by choice? Did they get to choose their sex at birth? Do they truly recognise their flaws in nature, or have they simply assumed they are perfect?

The truth is, no one has ever truly mastered or understood these aspects without consciously studying themselves through consistent, deep self-reflection.

Without Swadhyaya, a person remains unaware of their hidden ego, greed, fears, doubts and inner conflicts. They never truly realise how much hatred they carry in their heart or how much untapped potential they possess. Ironically, people only learn about their faults through others, which they instinctively deny. If someone points out their ego, they call it self-respect. If someone highlights their greed, they justify it as a necessity. If someone notices their doubts, they call it caution. In doing so, they spend their entire life trapped in misconceptions, false self-images, and layers of mistaken self-identity.

This is why Swadhyaya is essential for every human being. It acts as an internal health check-up, revealing the truth about oneself. Just as a medical test identifies hidden health issues before they become serious, self-study exposes inner flaws before they turn into lifelong limitations.

A person who truly knows themselves has the power to change, grow, and rise beyond limitations. This is the first step towards real success in life, aligned with Dharma.

When an individual does not dedicate even a little time to Swadhyaya, the real afflictions (Klesha) begin to take root. Klesha emerges when doubts replace confidence, hesitation suppresses initiative, and suffering dictates life.

Without Swadhyaya, a person becomes like a kite drifting aimlessly in the sky without a thread, a helpless deer wandering into a tiger's territory, or a small child lost in a complex neuroscience conference. Without Swadhyaya, a person moves through life like a headless chicken, constantly searching for answers but never truly knowing what they want, what they are capable of, and what their real purpose is.

Self-discovery is the true inventor of life, crafting the path from the soul within to the vastness of the universe beyond.

When a person lives under the weight of not knowing their inner complexities or their place in the outer world, Klesha takes hold on a large scale, leading to confusion, sadness, anxiety, analysis-paralysis and emotional turmoil.

Perhaps, Swadhyaya acts like a Google Map for the soul, helping navigate life's unknown territories with clarity and purpose. Just as a map prevents someone from getting lost in a new place, Swadhyaya helps a person understand themselves deeply, avoiding unnecessary suffering, conflicts, and hesitation in actions.

Saint Eknath was a great saint of Maharashtra who spent his life spreading devotion and wisdom. But his path was not easy. Society at that time was full of divisions, and many people did not accept his message of unity and Swadhyaya. He faced countless hardships, but he never let them shake his inner peace. One day, a man in a top position insulted him in public. He repeatedly spat on Saint Eknath, trying to provoke him. But Saint Eknath only smiled. Each time, he calmly walked to the river, washed himself, and returned without saying a word.

After many such insults, someone asked him, 'Maharaj, how come you don't get angry? Why don't you punish this man?'

Saint Eknath replied, 'He is spending his time in hatred, but I am using my time for patience. He is trapped in Klesha. His anger, pride, and ignorance are controlling him. But I have studied myself, and I know that anger will only harm me. Tell me, which is the better use of time?'

True peace arises when we understand ourselves and no longer allow the outside world to shake our inner stillness.

Always remember, the more we focus on the problems, the heavier they begin to feel and the more they seem to grow. But the moment we shift our thoughts towards possibilities, a new light appears in the form of an exit.

Klesha (hardship) not only affects a person's external world, but it also disturbs their inner peace. Imagine trying to use a complex gadget without knowing how it works. Imagine watching a suspenseful movie in a language you don't understand. Imagine playing a sport without knowing its rules. The frustration, awkwardness, and helplessness would be overwhelming. This is exactly how people live, constantly struggling, unaware of their own nature, habits, and emotional control.

This is why people burst into anger or lust and later regret it, promising never to repeat the same mistake, only to become angry again. They believe external situations or people are responsible for triggering their anger, but in reality, anger arises from within. The situation may act as a spark, but the fire burns within. Without Swadhyaya, they fail to recognise the patterns of their emotions and how these patterns control their responses. True peace originates from self-awareness, not from blaming others or circumstances.

Ironically, since people don't possess a deep understanding of themselves, they rely on others' opinions to define themselves. They constantly seek validation, asking how they look, how they performed, how skilled they are, or what they should do next. In reality, they are not seeking guidance; they are unknowingly searching for their own identity through the eyes of others. This search for self-understanding continues until the very end of life.

Every time we meet new people, we get surprised when they describe us in ways we never considered. Why is that so? Because we have never truly studied ourselves. We have overlooked Swadhyaya, and in doing so, invited Klesha into our lives. Understanding oneself is the only way to break free from the endless cycle of doubt and suffering. Only through Swadhyaya can a person truly find peace, clarity, and purpose.

A newborn's mind is a clean slate, except for the deep-rooted sanskara (past-life impressions). This is why even a toddler instinctively says, 'This is *my* toy.'

The 'I' factor emerges from past experiences and accumulated karmic influences. The ego a person nurtures in their current life does not end here; it carries forward, shaping future existences as well. Whether one believes it or not, this is the fundamental structure of the karmic cycle. So, do not hesitate or feel ashamed in accepting this ultimate truth.

It's we who divide experiences into good, bad, joyful, painful, and so on. When people experience something pleasurable, they wish to experience it again and again. That is why some people become addicted to drugs, habits, smoking, drinking, entertainment, or seeking constant company. However, in reality, trying to recreate the same experience is like a child wanting to relive the same excitement over and over. The first time, an experience may feel fresh and exciting, but the second time, it loses its novelty. Yet, people continue chasing that same feeling endlessly.

Understanding this truth aligned with Dharma is the first step towards wisdom. But people often hesitate to digest this bitter truth. A wise person realises that every life has a unique purpose, with its own strengths, weaknesses, and destiny. It is only our deep-rooted doubts that make us live in duality and analysis paralysis constantly, forcing us to overlook these aspects. Life will unfold as per its nature. That is why wise people first understand themselves and then accept life as it is, without complaints or regrets.

Logic may falter without roots, but the inner voice stands firm, timeless and true.

Life is about experiencing everything fully but never letting anything control us. Some days we get our favourite food and comforts, and some days we get nothing. It is up to us how we react to situations. Our actions and destiny shape our experiences. If everything happens as per our own karma and fate, then why complain? Who should we blame? Instead, we should embrace every experience and grow wiser from it.

This is the essence of wisdom: To accept life as it comes, learn from every experience, and move forward without attachment or expectation. That is how one truly lives a fulfilling and enlightened life.

One of my friends has spent forty-two years on this planet, still searching for the most basic questions—what should he do to achieve greater success? Which field suits him best? How can he become famous and rich? What will earn him respect and honour in society?

To find these answers, he attended countless personal development sessions, consulted numerous experts, and had deep discussions with friends and relatives he believed knew him well. He sought guidance from psychologists, astrologers, numerologists, and various occult scientists. He read hundreds of self-help books, watched hours of motivational videos on YouTube, and followed thousands of blogs. He attended seminars, workshops, and training programmes, all in the hope of finding the right path for himself.

But in reality, he was like a person wandering through a massive medical store, searching for a cure without even knowing his illness. Without understanding his real problem, he kept switching from one method to another, either continuously searching or constantly discussing, unaware that he had already spent half his life this way and was ready to spend the rest in the same confusion.

This is the purest form of Klesha, self-inflicted suffering born out of uncertainty, doubt, duality, and lack of self-awareness. It was not fate, nor society, nor circumstances that brought this Klesha into his life. It was his own decision, his own choice. Instead of chasing external answers, if he had turned inwards and embraced Swadhyaya, he would have found the clarity he sought. In that manner, he would have gained an understanding of his true self and core strengths.

Swadhyaya does not require endless searching. It requires a pause, a breath, a momentum of silence, a deep reflection, and the willingness to see oneself clearly.

It is the simplest yet most powerful process. Learning to say just two words to ourselves: 'Shut up!' Not to silence our voice, but to silence the endless chatter of doubt, hesitation, overthinking, and self-sabotage that keeps us trapped.

The mind is like a restless monkey, jumping from one thought to another, constantly questioning, analysing, fearing, and delaying. It creates a web of what-ifs, regrets, unnecessary comparisons, and imaginary problems that do not even exist. Every time we think, *what if I fail? What if I am not good enough? What if they judge me?* we need to stop, pause, and say, 'Shut up!'

The mind excels in hurting and wounding, but it hesitates when it comes to healing.

The Mahabharata is not just a tale of war but a treasure trove of wisdom. Several figures highlight the importance of Swadhyaya and the dangers of Klesha.

Yuyutsu was the son of Dhritarashtra, born to a Vaishya mother. He was raised in the Kaurava court and was expected to follow Duryodhana blindly. However, as the Kurukshetra war approached, Yuyutsu engaged in deep self-reflection. He questioned his loyalty and realised that his birth did not define his Dharma, but his actions did. Through Swadhyaya, he understood that supporting Duryodhana's unjust rule would only lead to ruin. On the eve of the war, Yuyutsu made the bold decision to switch sides and fight for the Pandavas. While all the other Kauravas perished, Yuyutsu was one of the few survivors, proving that self-awareness and the courage to act upon it can change one's destiny.

Similarly, after Lord Ram was exiled, Bharata was given the throne of Ayodhya. However, instead of accepting power blindly, he engaged in deep self-reflection. He asked himself: 'Am I truly worthy of the throne more than Lord Ram? What is my Dharma as a brother and as a king? If I take the throne, will I ever be at peace?' His Swadhyaya led him to reject the throne and rule Ayodhya as a caretaker, keeping Ram's sandals on the throne instead of himself.

On the other hand, Ashwatthama, Dronacharya's son, was a powerful warrior blessed by Lord Shiva, but his pride and anger blinded him. After losing the war, he gave in to hatred and killed the sleeping sons of the Pandavas—an act of deep Adharma. In return, Krishna cursed him with eternal life, filled with disease, pain, and loneliness. Burning with sorrow, Ashwatthama cursed back. He told Krishna he would die like a common man, alone in the forest, shot by a hunter. To Vyasa, he said his wisdom would be read but forgotten in times of darkness (Kaliyuga). Both curses came true. Krishna died alone, and Vyasa's teachings, though alive, are rarely followed.

In Jainism, Swadhyaya is a vital spiritual practice that leads to self-purification, right knowledge (Samyak Jnana), and ultimately, liberation (Moksha). It is considered one of the *Niyams* (essential duties) of a true seeker and is deeply connected to the core principles of Jain philosophy.

Additionally, engaging in self-reflection has been linked to improved mental health outcomes. A study conducted by Dr Harriet Demnitz-King and colleagues (2022) at University College London (UCL) found that individuals who practised self-reflection exhibited better cognitive function and healthier brain glucose metabolism, suggesting a protective effect against cognitive decline.

Thus, to read the scriptures without reading the self is like lighting a lamp outside while sitting in darkness within.

Exercise

Take a sheet of paper and write down the names of at least twenty people who you believe dislike you, envy you, have complaints against you, or hold unfulfilled expectations from you. Include those who criticise you behind your back.

Now, in front of each name, note down the flaws they see in you—whether it is ego, selfishness, arrogance, bad habits, harsh speech, greed, or any other bad trait.

Do this honestly, without making excuses for their such behaviour against you or adding any justifications.

Accept their perception as it is, without filtering it through your perspective. Remember, smoke only rises where there is fire.

Once you have listed everything, take a step back and see yourself from the world's viewpoint. Try to accept the truth without resistance. This is not about guilt or shame, but about self-awareness and transformation.

This is a form of Swadhyaya (self-study), a deep and honest self-reflection that every individual must practice at regular intervals. It helps us grow, both personally and professionally, making us stronger, wiser, and more evolved.

Dare to see yourself as the world sees you because only those who acknowledge their flaws can truly rise above them.

Key Takeaways

In the vast journey of human growth, one timeless practice shines with unmatched depth: Swadhyaya, the art of self-study. It is not just a reflection, but a scientific and disciplined method to understand oneself. Like a health check-up reveals hidden issues, Swadhyaya uncovers our mental patterns, emotional habits, and deep-rooted flaws. It demands honesty and courage, helping us recognise both our strengths and weaknesses. True growth comes not by rejecting imperfections, but by accepting and refining them with awareness, clarity, and the guidance of inner truth.

9

Atma Vivechan over Comparison

Purifying Within

आत्मानं रथिनं विद्धि शरीरं रथमेव तु।
बुद्धिं तु सारथिं विद्धि मनः प्रग्रहमेव च॥

One of the most valuable lessons from the Kathopanisad (1.3.3-4), this metaphor beautifully explains self-enquiry. If the mind (reins) is unsteady, the senses (horses) will lead us astray. However, if the intellect (the charioteer) is awakened through self-awareness, it guides us towards truth and inner stability. Through Atma-Vivechan (self-inquiry), one gains mastery over thoughts and emotions, leading to a balanced and enlightened life.

One of the most common yet unnoticed habits that almost every person falls into at some point in life is comparison. It may seem harmless, even natural, but it quietly becomes a childish way of feeding the ego. Without much effort, it gives a temporary feeling of being better or worse than someone else. Instead of helping us understand ourselves, comparison distracts us from our real path and makes us chase shadows that were never ours to follow.

When we fall into the habit of comparison, our mind becomes unusually active, sharp, quick, and focused, but sadly, not in the right direction. Rather than turning our attention towards those who can uplift us, guide us, or inspire us to grow, we often choose to compare ourselves with those who seem to be doing less or achieving slower. This isn't by accident; it's a careful, often unconscious choice that boosts our ego. We start believing that we are ahead, that our success is bigger, and that our life is more stable. But if we look closely, isn't this just a quiet form of self-deception?

Sometimes we fear the vastness of true success, so we settle quietly for the comfort of the small.

Just pause for a moment and reflect. Are we truly maturing, or merely building a false image to feel better about ourselves? Are we genuinely growing, or simply decorating our insecurities with borrowed pride? In the end, it is not the world that we are trying so hard to impress; it is our own restless mind that we are constantly trying to convince. And if we listen closely, beyond the noise of praise and judgment, somewhere deep within, we already know the truth we are trying to hide within.

Comparison has long been a silent destroyer, even in the greatest of stories. In Valmiki's Ramayana, when Lord Ram was about to be crowned king, Manthara quietly planted a seed of doubt in Queen Kaikeyi's heart. She compared Bharat's future with that of Lord Ram, whispering that Bharat would be reduced to nothing but a servant if Lord Ram ascended the throne. Until that moment of Adharma, Kaikeyi loved Lord Ram like her own son. But comparison twisted her love into fear and insecurity. It blinded her to the bigger picture and led her to demand Lord Ram's exile. The result was not just Ram's suffering; it brought sorrow to the entire kingdom of Ayodhya. A single comparison, born out of insecurity, changed the course of many lives.

Similarly, in the Mahabharata, during Draupadi's *swayamvara*, comparison silently played its part once again. When Karna stood up to try his skill, Draupadi, in a moment of pride, rejected him by calling him a *Sutaputra*, the son of a charioteer. It was not a judgement of Karna's ability or character, but a comparison based on birth and status. That small, cutting moment left a wound in Karna's heart that never fully healed. It was not just an insult; it was a reminder that no matter how talented he was, society would measure him against standards he could never change.

Both these examples teach us that comparison is not always loud and obvious. Sometimes, it is hidden in a single sentence, a passing thought, or an unexamined belief. Yet, it holds the power to change destinies. It creates divisions where there could be unity, and bitterness where there could be acceptance. True wisdom is in recognising this subtle danger and choosing to live by our inner values rather than by comparisons. Because real greatness is never built on proving others small, it is built on lifting oneself higher without pushing anyone else down.

Comparison is like a silent virus that slowly eats away at personal and professional flourishing. Yet, people continue to compare themselves to others, even when there is no logical basis for it. Despite knowing that every individual is as unique as their fingerprints, comparison has become an addiction. It is no longer limited to childhood rivalries; even grown adults engage in it repeatedly just to experience a fleeting sense of satisfaction. Perhaps, deep down, they are aware that their comparisons hold no real value.

Comparison is an art invented by fools, shaped by the losers, and practised by the immature.

This habit is much like drinking alcohol. A person knows that the effects of alcohol will wear off in a few hours, yet they consume it for temporary relaxation. Comparison, too, offers a brief illusion of comfort but ultimately leads to self-deception and wasted time. It does not contribute to growth or success; instead, it keeps us trapped in an endless cycle of self-delusion.

Doubt plays a crucial role in comparison. If a person dares to compare themselves with someone truly superior, they might find ways to improve, learning from those who have mastered their craft. However, this requires the courage to accept one's limitations, acknowledge failures, and embrace the effort needed to grow. However, doubts resist this process. It whispers excuses in our ears, convincing us that those at the top have unfair advantages or luck on their side. Instead of pushing us towards improvement, hesitation keeps us stuck in the comfort of mediocrity.

True growth begins when we stop measuring ourselves through the shadow of others and start seeing our worth in our own truth.

It is one of life's strange ironies that when we compare others, it feels right, even necessary. But the moment someone else compares us, we suddenly realise how painful, shallow, and foolish this game of comparison truly is. Yet, it remains one of the most favourite and hidden pastimes, not just for children, but for grown-ups, too. Like a secret sport, it is played in conversations, in silent thoughts, and even in fleeting glances, all in the endless search to feel greater than someone else. As if, by proving our superiority through comparison, the world would pause to build a statue in our honour!

Just picture who, in reality, has so much time to waste on such a meaningless act? These comparisons occur in the mind, in casual words, and in invisible thoughts, but rarely on the real grounds of action. And deep down, if we are honest with ourselves, we know that no true greatness has ever been born from measuring against others—it is born when we rise beyond it.

Comparison is a habit that, if left unchecked, can take over every aspect of life. I have a friend who has become so addicted to comparison that it is no longer limited to himself. He compares everything—his ten-year-old son with other children of the same age, his dog with other dogs, his furniture, mobile phone, mutual fund schemes, office cabin, car perfume, even his wife and parents. His mind is always preoccupied with comparing his life to others, which prevents him from finding peace in what he has.

Whenever he sees something better than his, he begins to curse it in the most creative ways, finding faults just to make himself feel superior. But if he finds something less impressive than his own, he expects praise. If people don't praise him, he reminds them repeatedly how his choices and decisions are far better. He does not rest until he hears appreciation. At times, he expects apologies from everyone.

Once we understood his habit, we found a way to make the most of it. We would praise him a little at first and then tell him, 'Let's go to a coffee shop, and we will tell you the rest of the praise there.' And surprisingly, he would take us to the coffee shop and pay the bill just to hear more about how brilliant he is compared to others. His need for validation was so strong that he didn't mind spending money on it.

It may sound extreme, yet the truth is almost everyone engages in comparison, a silent act that stands in quiet defiance of one's Dharma.

Maybe not as obsessively as my friend, but in subtle ways, we all do it. Some compare their careers, others compare relationships, wealth, or even social status in general.

The real question is, do we truly recognise this pattern within ourselves? Are we silently resisting the journey inwards? And more importantly, do we carry the courage to break free from this comfort of denial? The path to real wisdom begins the moment we stop fooling ourselves and start looking honestly at who we are becoming. It is not about being perfect, but about becoming a little more aware, a little more refined than who we were yesterday. For this, Atma Vivechan, or self-enquiry, becomes our guiding light. It is the inner process of tracing the root of our flaws, our habits, our emotional triggers, and understanding where they truly come from. Only when we go deep within with sincerity, not judgement, do we begin to transform, not just our behaviour, but the very foundation from which it rises.

Just as a tree draws its strength from deep roots hidden beneath the soil, our actions, mindset, nature, and the direction of our thoughts all rise from our inner self. For those who believe in the soul, it is seen as the foundation of all existence, the silent witness that never sleeps. And for those who do not hold such beliefs, they often turn to the mind as the centre of thought and identity. Yet, the real challenge lies not in belief or disbelief, but in the confusion that comes from comparison. In today's world, many unknowingly compare modern science with ancient spiritual wisdom, often without deeply understanding either. Science, though powerful, is still in its early stages when measured against the timeless vision of inner exploration offered by sages and scriptures. While science looks outwards, spirituality invites us to look within. Instead of competing, they can complement each other. But when we try to measure one with the tools of the other, we miss the essence of both.

Some people play the victim of circumstance, simply to escape the silent fear of being compared with the successful.

In the Mahabharata, when Indra approaches Karna in the disguise of a Brahmin to ask for his divine armour and earrings, Karna immediately senses that this is no ordinary request. Deep within, he recognises the identity of the visitor and the hidden purpose behind Indra's request. Yet, he does not react with anger, doubt, or fear. Nor does he boast about his giving nature. Instead, Karna withdraws into a quiet space within himself. He becomes still, not outwardly, but inwardly and reflects deeply on who he is, what he stands for, and what truly matters. It is not the pride of charity that drives him, nor the fear of losing his divine shield in an upcoming battle. In that sacred pause, he connects with his true self. He realises that his strength does not come from armour, but from his integrity. His choice to give away something so precious was not an impulsive act of heroism, but the outcome of his deep Atma Vivechan.

Atma Vivechan is the gentle art of tracing our thoughts back to their very roots. Since our thoughts quietly shape the direction of our lives, it becomes essential to watch them with care and honesty. We must learn to observe their patterns, notice their intensity, and understand how silently they guide our decisions and actions. When we develop this inner skill, we begin to gain true control over our emotions and our thinking. Slowly, we find ways to move beyond hesitation, doubt, and inner conflict, just like an experienced driver who, over time, learns to master even the roughest roads. Through Atma Vivechan, we stop being driven by our thoughts and lead them towards clarity, courage, and purposeful living.

Atma Vivechan is not merely a practice; it is a lifelong journey. It is the path to mastering our thoughts and emotions, breaking free from unconscious limitations, and evolving into a more fulfilled and enlightened version of ourselves. The more we engage in self-study, the more we realise that true growth comes not from comparing ourselves to others, but from understanding and improving the person we see in the mirror every day.

In the journey of professional success, the true achiever is the one who understands their core competency and natural potential. When a person aligns their actions with their true strengths, success becomes a natural outcome. No imitation can create true success, at best, it brings temporary recognition and short-lived returns. Real success comes only when a person is original in their ideas, methods, plans, working style, approach, attitude, mindset, and mentality.

The reason truly successful and wise people rise above the rest is simple—they dedicate more time to Atma Vivechan than anything else. They don't doubt ancient wisdom. They understand that true progress does not originate from external sources but from deep introspection. This habit of questioning oneself, analysing thoughts, and refining actions is what sets them apart from the crowd.

Yet in today's fast-moving world, many perceive Atma Vivechan as something outdated or unnecessary. They consider it an old idea, not suited for the modern age filled with instant information and digital advice. Instead of turning inwards, they turn to screens. They spend endless hours watching motivational videos, listening to powerful speakers, and following formulas that promise quick success. They want to rise fast, to succeed quickly, without pausing to understand who they truly are. But here lies the quiet irony—many of these people, who consume self-help content daily, often find it hard to bring any real change into their lives. They feel inspired for a moment, take notes, share quotes, but within days, they return to the same patterns, habits, and thoughts. The reason is simple. Without self-awareness, no inspiration lasts. Without inner clarity, no outer method works. Real transformation does not begin with external motivation, but with honest inner observation. Atma Vivechan is not old-fashioned; it is timeless.

The truth is that real success is not about growing faster but growing deeper. And this depth only comes through Atma Vivechan, where we stop chasing comparison and start discovering our true potential from within.

One of the stories from Uttar Kand of Ramayana suggests that Satyavrat, a righteous king, constantly compared his kingdom to others.

He often lamented, 'Why do other rulers have more wealth and prosperity while my land faces hardships?' Instead of focusing on his duties, he spent time envying neighbouring kings.

One day, a sage visited his court and advised: 'O King, a tree does not compare its height to another tree, nor does a river compare its flow to another. Each follows its natural path. Why do you not see that the role given to you is unique?'

Realising his mistake, Satyavrat shifted his focus from comparing to improving his kingdom. Over time, his land thrived not due to external competition, but through internal growth fostered by Atma Vivechan.

Neuroscientific studies show that self-reflection activates the prefrontal cortex, the part of the brain responsible for decision-making, problem-solving, and self-awareness. When we practice deep introspection, we train our brain to think critically about our progress rather than blindly comparing ourselves to others. This process reduces cortisol (the stress hormone), enhances cognitive flexibility, and fosters a growth mindset, a scientifically proven trait among highly successful individuals.

This delusion allows us to escape from what is most necessary, the honest self-evaluation of our thoughts and actions. However, the practice of Atma Vivechan begins when a person spends time in solitude and silence, engaging in deep self-reflection. It is about analysing every action, observing every thought that arises in the mind one after another, and categorising them: Which thoughts are pure? Which thoughts are impure? Which actions elevate me? Which actions degrade me?

Once this is identified, the next step is to take necessary actions to improve, refine, and transform those thoughts—the inner cleansing for outer transformation. Just as physical cleanliness freshens the body, mental and emotional purification through Atma Vivechan cleanses the soul. The changes made within eventually reflect in the outer world. A pure mind, a stable intellect, and a cleansed soul create a life of balance, clarity, and peace.

This is the beauty of Atma Vivechan, a process that transforms a person from within, leading to a life of true wisdom and Dharma, self-awareness, and personal and professional progress.

Exercise

Imagine you are taking a one-to-one counselling session for my friend, who always compares himself to others. You need to suggest ways and practices to help him break free from this habit. Keep it precise while considering the following points:

- Suggest Atma Vivechan (self-inquiry) in your own words as a solution to escape the comparison trap.
- Don't forget to use words like 'purpose of life', 'you can do it', 'success follows those who deserve it', 'life is priceless', 'time is short', and so on.

Once you finish writing, you will realise that the second option does not hold true in life; it only sounds good when spoken by motivational speakers. On the other hand, the first option reflects the true essence of self-inquiry and understanding.

Remember, when it comes to preaching, people often use grand words like those in the second option. However, when it comes to applying them in their own lives, they are filled with hesitation, excuses, and comparisons. So, suggest something practical, something you can genuinely apply in your own life to break free from this trap once and for all.

Key Takeaways

This chapter explores the deep power of Atma Vivechan, the timeless practice of self-enquiry. In today's modern world, it remains a practical path to inner clarity. Atma Vivechan helps shift focus from outer comparison to inner understanding. While we often measure our worth against others who seem more successful, this habit quietly harms our peace. True growth begins when we stop looking outward and start seeing ourselves through the clear mirror of awareness.

10

Shrota before Vakta

Advice and Consultation

विद्यां चाविद्यां च यस्तद्वेदोभयँ सह।
अविद्यया मृत्युं तीर्त्वा विद्ययाऽमृतमश्नुते॥

One of the most valuable lessons from the Isha Upanishad, Verse 11, it underscores the significance of discerning both knowledge and ignorance. For a 'Shrota' or seeker, it highlights the importance of understanding the material and spiritual realms. By attentively listening and comprehending these dual aspects, one can overcome mortal limitations and achieve eternal wisdom.

Among the greatest responsibilities in life is offering advice or giving counsel to others. When someone seeks our guidance, they place their trust in us, believing that our words will illuminate their path. However, if our advice is built on incomplete knowledge or half-truths, it can lead others towards confusion, suffering, or even destruction. In such a case, the burden of their downfall does not rest on them alone; it also belongs to the one who misguided them.

This is why it is our moral duty to pause and reflect before offering counsel. Are we truly knowledgeable in the subject we are advising on? Do we possess the real experience and in-depth understanding necessary to guide someone? If not, it is better to remain silent than to mislead another person.

However, true wisdom does not lie in speaking (Vakta) often or sounding intelligent. It lies in the quiet understanding that words aren't always needed, and silence holds greater power. A truly wise person does not speak to impress but to express what is necessary, helpful, or meaningful. They understand that silence can teach more than noise, and that, sometimes, holding back a word is a greater strength than delivering a clever sentence.

Yet, hesitation plays its trick on us simultaneously. Advising someone often makes us feel important—it boosts our ego, giving us an illusion of superiority. When a person seeks our opinion, we believe that we are the masters of that field, that our words hold authority. But have we ever stopped to check whether our wisdom is self-earned or merely borrowed? Have we gathered true experience, or are we merely repeating what we have heard from others?

After all, imitation is a monkey's business, and humans are meant to create, not copy.

A wise giver does not rush to donate without first ensuring that their own needs are met. Similarly, a true guide does not offer advice without first testing the truth of their own understanding. If we are quick to offer opinions but slow to verify facts, we must pause and ask ourselves if we are speaking from wisdom or simply reacting from ignorance. Before we open our mouths to guide someone else, we must first open our minds to honest self-reflection. Real guidance does not originate from a desire to impress or to sound intelligent. It comes from inner clarity, lived experience, and the humility to admit what we do not know. Our words carry weight, sometimes more than we realise. They can either light a path or leave someone lost. So, let us use them with care, with awareness, and with the quiet responsibility that true wisdom demands.

To become truly wise, one must first learn to listen. In ancient wisdom, the seeker is known as a Shrota (listener) before they can become a Vakta (speaker). There is a vast difference between these two. Similarly, there is a vast difference between Dharma and Adharma.

Real conversation begins not with words, but with the quiet grace of listening—where presence speaks louder than speech.

A Shrota is someone who gathers knowledge from every possible source with patience and humility. They absorb wisdom like the earth soaks in the rain, allowing it to settle deep within. On the other hand, a Vakta—or just a mind forever busy crafting thoughts—is someone who constantly seeks an opportunity to speak, to project their words, whether they possess the necessary understanding. It is important to note that being a Vakta is not inherently wrong, after all, a speaker has a vital role in society. But when a person speaks without first listening, without truly understanding, they become lost in the illusion of knowledge rather than its essence.

In today's world, nearly 90 per cent of people can be counted as Vakta, always eager to share their opinions, always searching for an audience. They take pride in speaking, mistaking it for wisdom. But only a rare 10 per cent are true Shrota, those who listen patiently—even to nonsense—without reacting impulsively. Their silence is more powerful than words. They speak only when it is truly needed because they understand that speaking is not merely about expressing thoughts, but it also consumes energy—both mental and physical. Even science confirms that excessive speaking leads to fatigue, while measured words conserve strength and clarity.

Always remember, when you speak less, your words carry more depth and power. In a world full of noise, silence adds value. Choosing your words carefully can touch hearts, create impact, and be remembered. Speaking less is not a sign of weakness; it is wisdom.

Words may whisper identities, but only actions aligned with Dharma unveil the truth of who we are.

A true Shrota, or a calm-hearted listener, listens without bias. They do not categorise information as good or bad but absorb what is useful, letting go of the rest. They do not argue unnecessarily or react out of frustration. In contrast, a Vakta feels an uncontrollable urge to respond to everything, even when the topic is irrelevant to them. They react impulsively, turning small matters into conflicts. While the Vakta is busy displaying his half-knowledge, the Shrota is quietly expanding his wisdom, learning more each day.

There is a certain hesitation that prevents a Vakta from accepting the limits of their knowledge. They speak confidently, believing that what they know is complete. A Shrota, however, watches such frequent talkers and understands how impatience blinds them. A true listener stays calm and observes, learning not just from words but also from people's behaviour, known as Vakta.

On the battlefield of Kurukshetra, Arjun stood not as a mighty warrior ready to fight, but as a man lost in emotion, doubt, and hesitation. His hands trembled, his bow slipped from his grip, and his heart was filled with confusion. But instead of reacting in anger or pride, Arjun made a choice that set him apart from an ordinary fighter. He became a Shrota, one who truly listens, not just with ears, but with silence in the soul. He sat before Lord Krishna with humility and full attention. For eighteen chapters, he did not interrupt or argue. He listened with an open mind, absorbing the wisdom of life, duty, and inner truth. It was this willingness to listen that changed him. He rose from uncertainty into courage, from inner conflict into clear action. He did not just fight a battle; he conquered the war within.

In the same spirit, the story of Nachiketa, the young son of Sage Vajashravas, as mentioned in the Katha Upanishad, carries a powerful lesson of Dharma.

When Nachiketa was sent to the house of Yama, the Lord of Death, he did not react with fear or frustration. Instead, he became a Shrota. He asked thoughtful questions about life after death, the nature of the soul, and the meaning of eternal truth. Yama tested him by offering riches and pleasures in place of answers. But Nachiketa remained calm and focused. He refused to be distracted. His strength lay in his ability to listen with patience and clarity. Seeing his determination, Yama finally shared the deepest secrets of life and immortality.

Both Arjun and Nachiketa teach us that true strength is not only in speaking or acting, but in knowing how to listen. Listening with attention and sincerity opens the door to real understanding. In a noisy world full of opinions and distractions, it is the quiet listener who often reaches the highest truth.

One of my friends has an in-built habit of advising everyone around him, as if he has appointed himself as a great Vakta while never truly embracing the role of a soul that absorbs.

His need to guide others is so strong that he rarely pauses to listen, believing that wisdom is only in speaking, not in understanding. Some of his funniest yet most common pieces of advice include lecturing people on financial planning while regularly borrowing money before salary, advising others to stay calm and control their anger, but losing his temper over slow internet, and passionately recommending books for self-improvement despite not having finished one in years.

He warns everyone about social media addiction yet checks his phone compulsively every thirty minutes. He preaches about work-life balance but takes office calls even at night, unable to disconnect. He even encourages people to take risks in life, yet hesitates while ordering food, unsure of what to order. He constantly emphasises the importance of listening but interrupts every conversation with his expert opinion. He criticises others for gossiping, yet starts every conversation with, 'Did you hear about her . . . ?' He gives business advice confidently but has never started one himself. He insists on the philosophy of going with the flow but overthinks even the smallest decisions in his own life.

Another challenge in becoming a listener with an empty cup lies in the hesitation to listen when the topic touches personal matters. Many people feel uncomfortable or even insulted when someone offers advice related to their own life. There is a silent doubt that accepting guidance might make them appear weak or dependent. As a result, they avoid open discussion, keep their struggles hidden, and resist seeking help.

On the other side, those who give advice often do so in a way that unknowingly carries a tone of superiority. Instead of creating space for understanding, their words make the listener feel judged or inferior. In such moments, guidance becomes a battle of egos rather than an exchange of wisdom. To awaken the true listener within, both humility in listening and sensitivity in speaking are necessary. Only then does advice become uplifting rather than uncomfortable.

In every meaningful conversation, a speaker and a listener hold the sky of wisdom together—each incomplete without the other. One listens to understand, and the other speaks to guide. But true listening is not just about hearing words, and true speaking is not just about sharing knowledge. A Shrota must carry the humility to receive without ego, while a Vakta must carry the responsibility to speak with truth, compassion, and clarity. When both roles are played with sincerity, wisdom flows naturally, without resistance or pride. The listener grows in awareness, and the speaker grows in responsibility. In this sacred exchange, learning becomes effortless, and transformation begins. Let us learn to listen not just with ears, but with an open heart. And let us speak not to impress, but to uplift. For when both the Shrota and the Vakta rise above their egos, real understanding takes root, and silence itself begins to speak.

Only those evolve and grow who speak less, listen deeper, and absorb the wisdom in silence.

Exercise

Choose a fine day for a simple yet revealing experiment.

Read something new and valuable, something unknown to most. Absorb its wisdom, then share it with as many people as possible in a day and observe how they react.

Some will listen patiently, others will interrupt, eager to add their own thoughts. Many will dismiss it, assuming they already know enough. This test will reveal a deep truth: Most people prefer speaking over listening.

But the real question is not about others, it is about you.

Do you truly listen when someone shares new knowledge? Or do you also wait for your turn to speak? Do you hesitate to accept wisdom that challenges your beliefs?

The world reflects who we are. As the wise say, one who knows himself fully can understand the whole world.

The mind resists listening, the ego defends itself, and hesitation blocks new learning. Yet, people chase perfection in life while holding onto these very flaws.

Awareness is the key. Observe, reflect, and most importantly, listen. True wisdom always begins in silence.

Key Takeaways

This chapter explores the power of listening, not as silence, but as the foundation of meaningful speech. Wisdom aligned with Dharma originates from the patience to listen and the desire to learn. Those who listen deeply and reflect sincerely speak with clarity and purpose. Their words carry weight, and their presence earns respect. But those who speak without understanding, and rush to share empty opinions, end up as noise heard, but never truly valued.

11

No Shoka, Only Anubhav

Overcoming Regrets

अनुभवो हि विशेषेण प्रमाणम्।

One of the most valuable lessons from the Vedantic and Nyaya Traditions, this explains that while scriptures, logic, and reasoning can provide guidance, true wisdom comes only through personal experience. No amount of theoretical knowledge can replace what is learnt through real-life trials.

Shoka means regret, and Anubhav means experience. Though both words may appear similar when seen in the context of life's journey, their essence is entirely different. Shoka comes from attachment to what could have been, from clinging to missed chances, broken expectations, or past mistakes. It drains energy and keeps the mind trapped in sorrow. On the other hand, Anubhav is the wisdom that arises from living through those very moments. It carries no blame, only learning. Where Shoka holds us back, Anubhav moves us forward. One binds us to the past with pain, while the other frees us with understanding. One binds, while the other liberates.

Regret (Shoka) is perhaps the most common emotion shared by all human beings. It does not discriminate between the rich and the poor, the young and the old, the educated and the uneducated. Almost every person walking on this planet, except a few enlightened souls, carries the burden of regret in some form. Life, for many, is nothing more than a collection of regrets, replayed over and over again in their minds. Even though people know that the past cannot be changed, they continue to live in its shadows, drowning in sorrow and deep pain.

This is why the world is full of songs about regret, movies about missed opportunities, and stories of people consumed by their mistakes. But rarely do we see stories that focus on true experience, on Anubhav, the raw and pure essence of life, without the weight of regret attached to it.

Regret adds nothing but more regret, wasting precious time in the act of regretting itself. It is the heaviest burden one can carry, not because of what has been lost, but because of what could have been. It is a silent companion of those who walk the path of ignorance, distraction, and fleeting pleasures, only to realise—when time has slipped away—that they had the power to live differently.

The Bhagavad Gita, the Garuda Purana, and other sacred scriptures are filled with profound lessons on how regret manifests when one fails to recognise the value of human birth, misuses the gift of time, or neglects responsibilities that shape not only this life but also the next.

Lord Krishna, in the Bhagavad Gita, reminds us that to be born as a human is a rare and divine opportunity, one that even celestial beings long for. It is in this form alone that one has the power to choose between wisdom and ignorance, righteousness and indulgence, self-realisation and self-destruction. But what happens when this sacred chance is wasted?

The Garuda Purana paints a haunting picture of the afterlife, where souls lament not over their material losses, but over the neglected duties. One of the greatest regrets a soul carries after death is the realisation that it failed to fulfil its responsibilities to parents, society, self-discipline, and righteousness.

Scriptures emphasise that duty is not just an obligation; it is the path to liberation and true Dharma. To perform one's duty, whether towards family, society, or the self, is to walk the path of righteousness. To neglect it is to accumulate regret that follows the soul beyond this life.

Similarly, the Brihadaranyaka Upanishad presents a beautiful analogy: If you try to explain the taste of salt to someone who has never tasted it, no words can capture its essence. But if that person tastes a grain of salt, the experience is immediate and undeniable. Similarly, one may read and discuss spiritual truths endlessly, but until one experiences them, they remain concepts, not reality.

The Mundaka Upanishad, too, states that a person can read a thousand books on fire, learn about its heat, its colours, and its chemistry, but unless they touch it, they will never truly understand fire. Similarly, one may read about meditation, devotion, self-discipline, or selflessness, but until they experience it, it remains second-hand knowledge.

History is filled with great figures who lived with Shoka, unable to escape its grip. King Dasharatha of Ayodhya, in a moment of love and gratitude, granted his wife Kaikeyi two boons. She later used them to demand Ram's exile, and in that single moment, the joyful life of the great king turned into unbearable sorrow. His greatest regret was not in keeping his promise, but in failing to see how that promise would shape his son's fate. He spent the last days of his life in misery, unable to accept what had already happened.

Julius Caesar, the great Roman ruler, also had his moment of Shoka. He trusted Brutus like a brother, never suspecting betrayal. But when Brutus turned against him in the final moments of his life, Caesar's last words, 'Et tu, Brute!' were not just an expression of betrayal, but of deep regret. The pain of being deceived by someone he trusted far outweighed the pain of death itself.

Shoka, or regret, is nothing but the feeling of failure, either due to inaction or hesitation. It begins as a simple doubt. However, over time, it grows into deep repentance. It keeps people trapped in their minds, making them relive the same mistakes repeatedly. Some carry their regret for days, some for years, and some for a lifetime.

The deeper we sink into regret, the more we silently lock a door that once led to tomorrow.

Hesitation is the root cause of most regrets. Either we hesitate to act when the time is right, or we act and later question why we did so. Instead of learning and moving forward, we remain stuck in the cycle of doubting our choices. Rather than overcoming these doubts, we allow ourselves to sink deeper into regret, living under its dark shadow.

But here lies a truth that must be accepted: There is no past, nor is there a future. Life exists only in the present moment. And life itself is nothing but a continuous series of experiences, called Anubhav. No one can hold onto these experiences forever. The problem begins when people label their Anubhav as good or bad, joyful or painful, worthy or unworthy.

Anubhav is just Anubhav—pure, unbound, and whole in itself, needing no category to be true.

Some experiences bring joy; others bring sorrow, and that is the natural rhythm of life. While a child cries for not getting what they want, many adults do the same when life doesn't meet their expectations. Is that not emotional immaturity? Life is like a beautiful painting made with many colours. If one insists on using only bright shades and avoids the darker tones, the picture will lose its depth and meaning. In the same way, wanting only happiness without accepting struggle takes away the true richness of living. Yet, when things don't go as planned, people slip into Shoka, letting regret cloud their vision. Every experience is shaped by the choices we make. When we take responsibility for those choices, we begin to replace sorrow with clarity and regret with real growth.

Thus, we must be careful with what is within our control. And for things that are beyond our control, the only wise response is acceptance. Acceptance of ourselves, of fate, and of Anubhav—without regret, hesitation, and fear.

Someone I know seems to love regret more than anything else in life. It has become his constant companion, chosen pastime, and strangely, a part of his identity. He wears his regrets like medals, not to heal from them, but to relive them. Over the years, he has mastered the habit of living in the past so well that people now offer him sympathy without him even asking, and he quietly enjoys the attention. While life keeps offering him new chances, he chooses to stay loyal to his sorrow. But experience is the ink with which the soul writes its evolution. We are meant to live, to learn, and to awaken. Regret may visit, but it should never be given a permanent seat.

Through sympathy, he gets to present himself as a poor guy, one who has been crushed by fate, tortured by circumstances, and beaten by the rest of the world. Every time I try to explain to him that regret serves no purpose and that he should move on, his response is always filled with deep hesitation. He insists that there is no way out of his sorrow, as if regret is a cage that has locked him forever. The amusing part is that some of his regrets are so minor that they hardly qualify as real suffering. Missing a train because of traffic is enough to send him into a spiral of sadness. Unlike most people, who only remember the major regrets of their lives, he has memorised every single one, as if collecting them like prized possessions.

If he could learn to live through Anubhav instead of holding on to Shoka, his entire life would change. Each day would feel like a new beginning, offering a fresh experience, a lesson, and a chance to grow without the weight of old sorrow. However, he is not alone. There are many people like him. Some express their sorrow through loud drama, making sure the world sees their pain. Others carry it quietly, letting it slowly eat away at their hearts and minds.

Regret is surely a painful emotion, but only until a person realises that whatever happened was the best that could be done with the understanding and awareness they possessed in that moment. Once this truth is accepted, regret begins to loosen its grip. The mind stops punishing itself, and the heart starts healing.

Just as life always offers us two choices in every situation, we also have a choice in how we carry our past. We can choose to live under the weight of regret, or we can choose to live with peace and blissfulness. We can either store Anubhav and grow through our experiences or hold on to painful memories and live in silent suffering. The choice is entirely ours. It depends on our wisdom and the foundational awareness of Dharma—on what we truly prefer, joy or pain. One single choice, one small decision, has the power to turn life around. It can shift us from joy to sorrow, or from sorrow to peace. Once we decide, with clarity and without doubt, we must walk that path with courage. Because in the end, life is not just what happens to us, but how we choose to respond, what we carry within, and what we leave behind.

Exercise

Take a moment. Pick up a piece of paper and write down this thought experiment. Imagine that you have discovered a time machine, a miraculous device that can take you back to the exact moment that has become your greatest regret. It is a chance to relive that moment, to go back in time and undo what went wrong.

But there is one condition; once you step into that moment, you will not remember anything about your regret nor any memory of the past incident. You will not know what mistake you made, nor will you have the wisdom to correct it. You will simply exist in that time, unaware of what went wrong or how to change it.

Now, ask yourself: Will this so-called boon truly help you? If you are unaware of what went wrong, how can you avoid repeating it?

This reveals a powerful truth: Regret does not exist in reality; it exists only in our memory. Regret is nothing but a loop in the mind, playing the same event repeatedly, making us believe that we are still suffering when, in reality, the moment is long gone.

This is how one overcomes Shoka and embraces real Anubhav. The art of living is not in returning to the past but in choosing how to remember it. It is not in erasing mistakes but in learning from them without carrying their burden.

Key Takeaways

Regret is a futile emotion that drains time and energy, causing unnecessary suffering without offering solutions. Dwelling on the past changes nothing; it only prolongs the pain. The key to overcoming regret is shifting full focus to the present. While acknowledging past experiences is important, one must not be defined by them. True growth arises from directing energy towards creating a better future rather than reliving the mistakes.

12

Abhay

The Mark of a Winner

अभयं सत्त्वसंशुद्धिर्ज्ञानयोगव्यवस्थितिः।

One of the most valuable lessons from the Bhagavad Gita (16.1), Lord Krishna describes the qualities of a person who follows the divine path. The first quality mentioned is *Abhayam* (fearlessness), which signifies complete freedom from fear, doubt, and anxiety. True fearlessness emanates from inner purity, self-knowledge, and unwavering faith in Dharma. When a person aligns with higher wisdom and truth, fear automatically disappears.

Bhay (fear) is a natural emotion. It is built into the human mind as a survival tool, which is why it becomes an unavoidable part of life. However, it becomes problematic only when it turns into hesitation and stops us from moving forward. The truth is that fear stays strong only until we gather the courage to face it. The moment a person accepts the situation as it is, without resistance or denial, and chooses to act with strength, fear begins to fade.

Acceptance brings clarity, and with clarity comes confidence. Once we stop running from fear and start walking through it, its power over us begins to disappear.

Doubt and fear are like shadows that follow each other closely. When fear enters the mind, doubt quietly follows, questioning every step, every decision. And when hesitation takes hold, fear becomes even stronger, feeding on that uncertainty. It is like walking through a dark alley at night—the moment a person hesitates or looks back, fear begins to rise, and the darkness feels deeper and more frightening. But if one walks forward with steady steps and a clear mind, the same darkness begins to lose its power. What once felt terrifying appears manageable. In truth, fear is not always present *in* the situation; it often lives in the way we think. When doubt leaves, courage enters, and even the darkest path becomes walkable.

Our deepest fear lies in knowing that the world silently waits for our fall.

Ravana's wife, Mandodari, fears the destruction her husband's ego will bring. She warns him to return Sita, fearing not only war but the moral collapse of Lanka. Her fear is quiet and rooted in wisdom, but Ravana's refusal to listen leads to tragedy. Here, Mandodari shows that fear voiced with love can be a form of moral courage.

Fearlessness has always captured human imagination. It is why certain moments in cinema remain unforgettable. The intense docking scene from Interstellar, the grand entry of Pushpa, the throne ceremony of Bahubali, and the powerful presence of Rocky Bhai in KGF, all these moments became iconic because they portrayed absolute fearlessness. Audiences felt an unshakeable admiration because deep down, everyone desires to be like that, to stand strong, to face challenges without hesitation, to live without fear.

The truth is, Abhay, fearlessness is about choosing courage despite fear—Dharma over Adharma. The moment a person stops doubting and takes action, fear has no place to exist. That is when life is truly lived, not as a sheep that follows, but as a lion that leads.

Lord Ram is the embodiment of Abhay. Whether facing exile, walking through the forest with no complaint, or standing alone against Ravana, he remains calm, steady, and clear in his purpose. His fearlessness does not come from physical strength alone, but from the inner strength of Dharma. Even when he loses Sita, Lord Ram does not break down in fear. He gathers his strength and moves ahead with faith and action. His Abhay is not noisy; it is graceful, patient, and deeply rooted in inner clarity.

Once a person truly understands that life presents only two outcomes—victory or defeat—the fear of failure loses its grip. The mind becomes free from unnecessary doubts, allowing actions to flow without fear. However, one must be cautious not to fall into the trap of trying to prove something to others through success or failure.

Success gained through Adharma is a hidden loss, while failure earned through Dharma is a victory beyond all measure.

Life is not a stage for external validation. It is not about demonstrating superiority to people, nor is it about seeking approval from the world. Victory and defeat are merely milestones in the journey of Anubhav—experiences that shape growth. Beyond these external results, what truly matters is a person's commitment to their Dharma and Kartavya, their duty and responsibility.

When a person acts with this mindset, fear disappears completely. There is no need to win for applause or fear losing for criticism. What remains is pure action, free from hesitation, guided by a sense of duty. This is the true essence of Abhay—a state where neither victory nor defeat define a person, but their unwavering commitment to their path does.

The brave Jatayu shows Abhay when he fights Ravana to protect Sita. Though he knows he cannot win, he still gives his all. He does not fear death. His body may have fallen, but his spirit became immortal. He teaches that true Abhay is not about success, but about standing up for what is right, even if it costs the most precious.

The story mentioned in the Nath Sampradaya, Matsyendranath, one of the founders of the Nath tradition, was swallowed as a baby by a giant fish and ended up in the depths of the ocean. Inside the belly of the fish, he overheard Lord Shiva teaching Parvati the secrets of yoga and immortality. Instead of being terrified, he remained fearless and absorbed the teachings. When the fish was eventually caught by fishermen, Matsyendranath emerged as a fully enlightened yogi. He became a master of Hatha Yoga, proving that Abhay is achieved through self-realisation and inner wisdom.

In every heart, there exists a shadow, a silent tremor that shapes our actions and thoughts. This shadow is fear. Some fear losing their loved ones, while others fear losing their jobs, status, wealth, or authority. Some worry about setbacks in their careers, losses in the share market, or even something as small as a scratch on their car. Some fear growing old, looking unattractive, or being judged by others. Many fear that life will not unfold the way they wish.

Life, for most, becomes a long journey lived under this fear. But where does this fear come from? It is not something external; it is born within us, nurtured by our doubts, hesitations, and dualities. It is the mind's creation, a cloud that keeps us from seeing the clear blue sky of our true self.

Yet, beyond this shadow, there exists a different state of Abhay—a fearless existence. To live without fear is the true achievement of life, oriented with Dharma.

The fear of losing status, position, or wealth is also an illusion. One day, we all have to step down, retire, or move on. Clinging to temporary things with fear only makes the departure more painful. Instead, if we accept that change is the nature of life, we walk with graceful Anubhav, the purest form of Dharma.

Of all the fears we carry, the fear of judgement serves us least, for it dims our light to please eyes that may never truly see.

Think deeply, how many people truly have the time to judge you all the time? Each person is busy with their own struggles and worries. If someone does judge you, let them be the judge. Why must you stand in their court as an advocate defending yourself? The world will talk, and the world will forget. The drama of fear will continue as long as we resist the flow of life. The moment we embrace life as it is, surrender to its rhythm, and walk with Abhay, fearlessness becomes our companion. It is then that we become light like a feather, untouched by the winds of worry, and filled with deep, unshakable peace.

Abhimanyu, just sixteen, chose to enter the deadly *Chakravyuha* knowing he might not return. With no hesitation, he stepped in when others held back. Surrounded and attacked unfairly, he fought alone with unmatched courage. His fearlessness was not loud, it was calm, clear, and purposeful. Abhimanyu shows us that true Abhay is not in avoiding fear, but in standing firm despite it. His short life became a timeless lesson in bold action and inner strength.

Fear is a natural emotion, meant to protect us, but over time, it begins to control us. Psychology explains that fear takes different forms, shaping our thoughts and actions in ways we often don't realise.

Some fears are innate, present from birth, like the fear of loud noises or sudden movements, designed to keep us safe. Others are learnt, picked up through life experiences, fear of failure, rejection, or past traumas that leave lasting marks.

Then come social fears—the fear of judgement, embarrassment, or not being accepted, making people hesitate even when they have something valuable to share. The most extreme are pathological fears or phobias, like the fear of open spaces, closed rooms, or heights, which can take over a person's life completely.

Fear, when uncontrolled, becomes a cage. But no fear is permanent. The moment we recognise it and stop running from it, its power weakens. Fear is just a shadow, and like every shadow, it disappears when we bring in the light of courage and awareness. That is when true freedom, true Abhay, begins.

80 per cent of our past fears never came true, yet the mind keeps weaving new ones and we, the innocent, keep joining the fear party, again and again.

Duryodhana, the eldest of the Kauravas, spent his entire life fearing the strength and Dharma (righteousness) of the Pandavas. Instead of overcoming this fear through wisdom, he allowed it to control his actions. His fear made him insecure, and his insecurity made him resort to deceit and war. Even when offered peace, Duryodhana's fear of losing power led him to reject all solutions. His refusal to face the truth and his blind arrogance, which was born out of fear, led to the destruction of his entire family. If he had conquered his fear and made peace, history would have been different. But fear, when not controlled, turns into destruction.

Sage Tulsidas, in his boundless wisdom, gave the world a simple but powerful truth through his words: '*Tulsi bharose Ram ke, nirbhay hoke soye, Anhoni honi nahi, jo hona so hoye.* [One who has faith in Lord Ram sleeps without fear, because they know that what is meant to happen will surely happen, and what is not meant can never harm them.]'

This simple yet deep truth, as shared by Tulsidas, teaches us that life is not meant to be lived in fear or anxiety. When we trust the divine plan, we stop worrying about the future or regretting the past. We start living with calmness in the present, knowing that everything will unfold as it is meant to. Such faith brings inner peace and strength in every moment.

Exercise

Take a moment and write down the biggest fears you have experienced in life so far. Recall the times when you were anxious, when you thought something terrible would happen. Now, compare those fears with reality. How many of them turned out exactly as you had imagined?

Most people realise that at least half of their fears never came true the way they thought they would. Some vanished with time, some changed form, and some were never as dangerous as they seemed in their mind. Yet, despite knowing this, we continue to create new fears about our future.

Now, if you were to write five fears about your future, pause and ask yourself, 'Will they happen the way I am imagining, or will they unfold in their own way, as life intends?'

This simple exercise reveals a great truth. Fear is not real; life does not unfold according to our fears; it follows its own rhythm. Understanding this truth is the first step towards living in Abhay, the fearless state of being.

Key Takeaways

Fear shapes our thoughts and actions, often making us believe in the worst possible outcomes. However, when we look back at our biggest fears, we realise that many never happened the way we imagined. The realisation helps us understand that life unfolds in its own way, beyond our fearful projections. The key to Abhay, or fearlessness, is to stop giving unnecessary power to fear and trust the natural flow of life.

13

Satya over Kalpana

Living in Reality

सत्यं शिवं सुन्दरं नानृतं नापि कल्पना।
सत्येन धार्यते विश्वं न कल्पनया कर्हिचित्॥

One of the most valuable lessons from the Mundaka Upanishad (3.1.6) reveals that truth is auspicious and beautiful, while falsehood and imagination hold no real value. The universe is sustained by truth, never by mere imagination.

The Brihadaranyaka Upanishad (1.4.14) teaches that nothing is higher than Dharma, and this Dharma is Satya, the eternal truth. Truth is not only in words but in the unity of thought, speech, and action with reality. Kalpana, the mind's imagination, can create beauty but also weave illusions that hide the real. Satya stands beyond these changing images—constant, pure, and free from desire or fear. To live by truth is to live in harmony with the cosmic order. Kalpana may shape our dreams, but Satya shapes our destiny.

Imagination is the bridge that connects the seen world with the unseen depths within us. Satya, the truth, and Kalpana, the illusion, are not unfamiliar words. You have heard them before, perhaps even spoken of them. But have you ever paused to feel how they quietly grow inside you? How they shape your thoughts, influence your choices, and colour your understanding of life? Satya brings clarity, while Kalpana paints possibilities, both silently shaping your reality. To know them not as ideas, but as living forces within, is where real understanding begins.

Modern medical science tells us that the heart is merely a pumping machine, a physical organ with no sensory functions. If that is true, then what remains is the mind, the invisible force that directs our behaviour, emotions, and beliefs.

But here lies the real mystery. The mind, when it is born, knows nothing. It enters the world as a blank page, carrying only the basic instincts needed to survive. It does not accompany wisdom; it gathers knowledge through the five senses. Whatever it sees with the eyes, hears with the ears, smells, tastes, or touches, it accepts as real. In this way, the mind becomes completely dependent on the outer world to decide what is Satya and what is Kalpana. It does not question at first; it simply absorbs. And because of this dependence, the line between truth and illusion blurs, shaped not by inner clarity but by external influence.

If the mind is dependent, then it becomes our sacred duty to nourish it with the truth of Satya and the path of Dharma, not the illusions of Kalpana.

In the book of life, Kalpana may fill a chapter, but Satya will always be the title that lasts.

Truth, or Satya, is the foundation on which real existence stands. It holds the deep mysteries of life, the purpose behind our journey, the values by which life is meant to be lived, and the timeless wisdom preserved in scriptures and ancient teachings. Satya is not created; it simply is. It does not depend on opinion or approval. It remains steady, whether accepted or not. On the other hand, Kalpana, or illusion, has no solid ground beneath it. It is born from incomplete knowledge, misunderstandings, doubts, and the stories we create in our minds. Sometimes, it is celebrated as imagination, creativity, or vision, but in truth, Kalpana is only a series of thoughts built on uncertain ideas. It may appear beautiful or inspiring, but it often floats without roots, disconnected from what actually exists. While imagination has its place, when mistaken for truth, it becomes a shadow that distracts us from reality. Recognising the difference between Satya and Kalpana is the first step towards living with clarity.

Let's take a simple example. Picture a purple tiger. Have you ever seen one? No. Still, if I ask you to picture it, your mind will create an image of a tiger with purple fur. How does this happen?

The mind, being filled with Ahankara (ego), does not want to admit that it does not know a purple tiger. So instead, it does what it always does—it takes the concept of a tiger and the colour purple, merges them, and presents it as something that feels real. But is it real? No. It is just a Kalpana, a projection of the mind which is not Satya.

This is how illusion works. The mind does not always differentiate between what is real and what is imagined. If given the wrong input, it will believe in falsehood as easily as it believes in truth.

Consider another example: Tell a ghost story to a child and watch their reaction. Even though they have never seen a ghost, they start believing in it. The fear in their eyes, the way they hesitate to enter a dark room, the way they suddenly feel unsafe in a place they have lived for years—all of this happens because their mind has accepted the illusion. They live in fear of something that does not even exist. This simple example proves a powerful truth: The mind only works with what is given to it.

This is why our ancient scriptures insist on feeding the mind with truth, not illusions, with Dharma, not Adharma. The sages and rishis did not waste time in stories of imaginary creatures or false fears. They focused on absolute knowledge. The eternal principles of life, the workings of the universe, the science of existence. But today, many people prefer Kalpana over Satya.

One of my friends is exactly like this. He questions everything that comes from ancient wisdom and rejects anything that is not scientifically proven. Whenever I share with him that our scriptures hold deep knowledge in areas like economics, astronomy, mathematics, physics, health, occult sciences, and geography, he immediately dismisses it. His reply is always the same. If science has not confirmed it, he will not believe it.

One day, I asked him a simple question, 'If I tell you that my stomach is aching, how will you know what I am going through?'

He paused for a moment and replied, 'I will remember how it felt when I had a stomach ache and try to understand what you're feeling.'

That was the moment I made my point. He cannot measure my pain in kilograms, litres, metres, or any scientific unit. He cannot write a formula to prove how much it hurts. My pain is my direct experience, real and undeniable to me. His understanding, however, is based on assumptions, memory, and imagination. In this case, my pain is Satya, the truth I am living, while his understanding of it is Kalpana, an illusion shaped by his own limited experience. This is the difference between true knowledge and assumed knowledge. Not everything real can be weighed, tested, or labelled. Some truths must be felt, lived, and realised, not proved.

This is how Satya and Kalpana operate in life. Remember, truth is not to be found outside, but to be realised within.

Have you ever wondered how the mind weaves illusions so convincingly that people begin to accept them as truth? Through Kalpana, the imagination of the mind, Maya takes form and spreads its net around us. This Maya is not something distant or unseen; it is present in the everyday beliefs we hold, in the things we accept without questioning, and in the way we live our lives without realising that much of it is an illusion.

When the heart knows the wrong yet wears it as a crown, it is the first thread in Maya's endless weave.

Look at the world around you, and you will see this illusion at play. People say that money is everything, that it has the power to buy happiness. Some believe that winning is the only thing that matters and that losing is equivalent to the end of life. Yet, history shows that those who once lost are the ones who later rose to greatness. Some say that growing older means becoming wise, but does age alone guarantee wisdom? If that were the case, then wouldn't every old person be enlightened? Then there is the belief that knowledge is more powerful than wisdom, that collecting information is more important than understanding it. But if knowledge alone were the ultimate power, wouldn't those who memorise facts be the wisest? Similarly, many believe that information is greater than experience. They think that reading about something is the same as knowing it, that hearing about a river is the same as swimming in it. But can the taste of a fruit ever be understood just by reading about it?

The illusion does not stop there. People often place imagination above reality, as if thinking about something is more important than actually experiencing it.

They believe that words alone hold the power of expression, that having a large vocabulary is more important than knowing how to communicate with the heart. But true communication is not about using difficult words; it is about making someone feel understood.

In the Ramayana, Sita, too, becomes a victim of Kalpana when she sees the golden deer. Her desire for the beautiful creature makes her forget the dangers around her. She imagines the deer to be harmless and demands that Ram bring it for her. But this small illusion opens the door for Ravana to enter. Later, Ravana himself lives in Kalpana when he believes that he can win over Sita by force and that no one can defeat him. His pride blinds him to the truth of Ram's strength and dharma. In all these moments, Kalpana overshadows Satya, leading to downfall.

Kalpana is a state of mind where a person believes that something unreal is real. It is a mirage that keeps one trapped in an imaginary world, distancing them from what truly exists. This deception does not just reflect in personal thoughts but also in ideologies, ethics, rules, and moral principles. The mind, by its very nature, is like a factory, constantly producing thoughts, sometimes driven by desires, sometimes by revenge, sometimes by worry, and often by pure fantasy. It does not give even a moment of rest, pulling a person into a never-ending cycle of past regrets and future anxieties. In this restless movement, one remains suspended between Kalpana (illusion) and Maya (delusion), while Satya (truth) gets left behind.

Yet, those deeply caught in this Kalpana hardly realise they are trapped. The power of Maya is such that even when people live in their imagined worlds, they deny its existence. Just as a child believes that Superman and Spiderman exist somewhere in reality, adults, too, get convinced that their false beliefs, assumptions, and dreams are real. But just as a dream vanishes the moment one wakes up, Kalpana dissolves when Satya is realised.

Doubt often becomes the biggest obstacle in discovering Satya. It is because reaching the truth requires effort, patience, and continuous self-discipline. The path to Satya is not easy; it demands courage to accept reality as it is. On the other hand, Kalpana is effortless; it does not require any struggle, only submission to the illusions created by the mind. That is why people naturally lean towards Kalpana instead of seeking Satya.

Seeking Satya is like becoming a billionaire; everyone desires it, but only a few truly work for it.

Many people live not by truth but by Kalpana, mental illusions shaped by fear, assumptions, and incomplete understanding. These illusions feel real but are not based on Satya. Common examples include beliefs like 'I will be happy when I achieve more', 'Others' opinions define my worth', or 'Life is unfair when things go wrong.' People avoid pain, thinking it is wrong, chase success, believing it lies in fame and wealth, and delay change, thinking time is always available. But real happiness lies in the present, self-worth arises from within, and every experience teaches something. Spirituality does not remove pain; it provides us with the strength to face it. The past does not define us; our choices do. Simplicity often brings more peace than excess. And no one is truly alone in their struggle. Moving from Kalpana to Satya is a shift from confusion to clarity. This shift brings inner strength, freedom, and true peace.

The world of cinema has beautifully portrayed this conflict between Kalpana and Satya. Take the movie *Inception*, where Cobb constantly struggles to distinguish between dream and reality. He is haunted by guilt and lives in a state of doubt, unsure whether he is awake or still inside a dream. But when he finally accepts the truth, he understands the real nature of his existence.

Similarly, in the movie *Tamasha*, Ved follows the societal script, living a Kalpanic life, thinking that it is his true purpose. But when he emotionally breaks down, he realises his Satya, that his real passion is storytelling. The moment he accepts it; he transforms and rises.

Satya is the highest state of inner clarity, where all illusions slowly dissolve. It is the point where hesitation fades away and one discovers true Abhay. A person who realises Satya no longer gets carried away by passing thoughts, emotions, or momentary desires. Such a person walks steadily on the path of Dharma, living with purpose, honesty, and peace. But to reach this state, one must gather courage, break free from the web of Kalpana, and accept the truth as it is, not just what is convenient to believe. Satya is not something that changes with time. It is the reality that was, is, and will always be. Only when one chooses to face it with open eyes and a strong heart does real transformation begin.

Exercise

This exercise requires observation, inquiry, and reflection. First, identify two categories of individuals. First, the self-made individual, a person who has built their wealth and success through perseverance, struggle, hard work, and real-world experience. And second, a person who has been born into financial privilege and has never personally experienced the journey of wealth creation.

If possible, engage in a personal conversation with both individuals and ask them the following questions:

- What does it take to achieve wealth and success?
- What is the formula for success according to you?

Now, carefully analyse their answers and note the difference in their perspectives. Pay attention to the depth of their responses, the elements of effort and experience, and whether their answers are practical or theoretical.

The self-made individual may likely emphasise hard work, discipline, failures, and resilience as the essential ingredients of success. Their insights will be deeply rooted in Satya, as they have lived through the reality of struggle and achievement.

In contrast, an individual born into wealth may attribute success to factors such as luck, mindset, networking, or vague principles, often lacking personal struggle or direct experience. Their perspective may be more aligned with Kalpana, shaped by inherited circumstances rather than earned wisdom.

By completing this exercise, you will gain a deeper understanding of the fundamental difference between Satya and Kalpana.

This realisation applies not only to wealth but to all aspects of life. Whenever you hear someone advising on success, happiness, or purpose, ask yourself: Are they speaking from lived experience, or are they merely assuming? Recognising this distinction will bring clarity, wisdom, and a deeper connection to reality.

Key Takeaways

Satya is about truly living with awareness, while Kalpana traps us in illusions. When one seeks Satya, hesitation creates inner conflict, and Maya strengthens those doubts. Yet, no illusion can ever replace truth. A person may keep imagining and dreaming, but Satya remains unchanged. The moment one dares to face it; illusions fade and peace returns. Life is meant to be lived in truth, not wasted in fantasies. The choice is ours to stay in Kalpana or walk the path of Satya and Dharma.

14

Bhava Santulan

Moving on from Moha

मोह एव महामृत्युः मोहो मृत्योरपत्यकम्।
मोहो हि बन्धनं पुंसां मोहो वै निश्चलं तमः॥

One of the most valuable lessons from the Mahabharata (Shanti Parva 177.22), where Bhishma explains the dangers of Moha to Yudhishthira, Moha (attachment) is the greatest form of death, a child born out of death itself. Moha binds human beings and keeps them trapped in illusion. It is nothing but dense, unmoving darkness that prevents one from seeing the truth.

Moha does not simply mean love or care. It is a binding attachment that clouds right thinking. It leads to an individual becoming emotionally attached to things, people, ideas, and positions in such a manner that they lose clarity, balance, and objectivity. Under the influence of Moha, one becomes overly attached to outcomes, refuses to accept change, and suffers when life does not go as expected.

If given a choice, many would rather face death than share even a small part of their wealth with society. They fight long legal battles against their family members over property, refusing to let go of what they believe belongs to them. When it comes to charity, most people offer coins to beggars as if they were created only for the poor. Offering a currency note feels excessive, as if giving more would break some hidden social rule. This is not about the money but the mindset. The unwillingness to give, the tight grip over wealth, and the fear of letting go—especially in small acts—reveal how deeply material possessions control the mind. True generosity is not about the amount; it is about the heart behind the act. In such moments, the need for Bhava Santulan, or emotional balance, becomes clear. It means balancing the self from within, especially from attachments that bind us. When we are not affected by gain or loss, by praise or blame, and when we remain steady in giving and living, we begin to experience inner balance. That is the true Bhava Santulan, where one lives with freedom in this life and walks lighter into the next.

Life after life, the soul watches its own stories unfold—each like a film with a changed cast, altered stories, and an ending only eternity knows.

Everywhere you look, Moha has silently taken hold of human hearts. People today find it extremely difficult to part with anything, whether it is wealth, knowledge, time, or even basic resources. The same individuals who lose lakhs in the stock market, who bear major losses in business without hesitation, or who spend freely on their habits and luxuries, suddenly become silent or defensive when asked to help someone in need.

When a struggling person reaches out for support, they are not met with understanding but long speeches on discipline, hard work, and success. These words ignore the deeper truths of life, such as helpless situations, karma from past actions, and painful circumstances that push a person into misery. This shows how deeply Moha controls the mind. It blocks generosity and replaces empathy with judgement. To rise above Moha is not about giving up everything but about opening the heart to share, to understand, and to serve when it truly matters.

Moha is not limited to attachment towards wealth alone. It quietly extends its hold over many aspects of life. People become attached to power, relationships, beliefs, addictions, habits, positions, authority, a sense of superiority, dignity, and even their own false perceptions.

It is this invisible grip of Moha that clouds the mind and closes the heart. Under its influence, individuals fail to see the larger truth that the world is interconnected, and every person is simply living their karma. When Moha takes over, the focus shifts from understanding to control, from compassion to possession. To break free from Moha is to see life with clarity, to accept change, and to understand that freedom comes not from holding on, but from letting go with wisdom.

Sometimes, letting go is not a defeat;
it is the beginning of a greater victory within.

Moha, the highest form of Adharma, is so deeply rooted in human nature that people become attached to almost everything. Some are bound to their addictions, believing them to be their strength, while others cling to their careers, relationships, power, clothes, pets, cars, gadgets, and even the smallest of material possessions. It does not matter whether the object of attachment is expensive or cheap—once Moha takes hold, it blinds a person to their soul.

Moha is nothing but another form of greed. And greed has no limit. It is like a vast ocean; no matter how much water is poured into it or taken away, it remains unchanged.

Similarly, no amount of wealth, success, or possessions can satisfy a person driven by Moha. The hunger only grows, burning away life from both ends, leaving no space for peace or contentment.

A hesitant and doubtful mind is its biggest ally. The one who doubts letting go of attachment, who constantly fears loss, who refuses to see beyond possessions, is the one who remains trapped in Moha. The more one holds on, the deeper the suffering becomes. The only way to free oneself is to recognise that nothing truly belongs to us, not our wealth, not our relationships, not even our own bodies. Everything is temporary. But only those who dare to accept this truth can walk the path of real freedom.

True Bhava Santulan teaches us that life is meant for experience. It enlightens us with the true sense of Dharma. Everything that comes our way exists only for Anubhav. Nothing in this world is permanent. Age, skin, beauty, status, wealth, and identity will all fade with time. Everything we hold on to today will one day turn to dust. This simple awareness can change the way we live. It teaches us to live like a feather—light and free. Once we realise this truth, we will enjoy every moment fully, whether it is joyful or painful, because we know it will not last forever. This bhava (understanding) changes our perception, brings peace, and reduces emotional burden.

As Moha fades into silence, the soul awakens to the breath of Bhava Santulan.

A king once asked a wise writer to write something that would bring comfort during suffering and also remind him of the truth during moments of great joy.

The writer simply gave him one sentence: 'This, too, will pass soon.'

That one line holds the heart of Bhava Santulan. Everything changes. Joy and sorrow, gain and loss, success and failure, all are passing clouds. Therefore, we must create this life with a meaningful sense, by lifting others when we have the opportunity and sharing joy with those who have less or nothing. Life becomes richer not by accumulation but by contribution. Just as some of the world's most successful individuals, like Bill Gates and Warren Buffett, took the initiative to pledge a major part of their wealth to humanity, we must find our way to give back as well—whether through time, effort, knowledge, or resources.

Moha is like an endless thirst. No matter how many Pizzas a person has eaten in life, they still desire to eat more. A person may have smoked thousands of cigarettes, yet the craving for the next one does not stop. Someone may have earned crores, yet the desire to earn even more never lets them rest. Moha keeps a person unsettled, both in personal and professional lives. It keeps the mind chasing without peace. To find balance and fulfilment, one must first recognise this never-ending grip and slowly step out of it with awareness.

That is why Bhava Santulan, the art of self-balance, must be learnt by all, not to become someone special, but to become truly human.

Life is like a game, with built-in challenges and imperfections. The rules are simple—every person is born with flaws, including Moha, and the task is to overcome them. Those who succeed in breaking free from their attachments and other flaws win the game. Those who fail must continue playing, life after life, returning in different forms with new possibilities but carrying the same core flaws.

To help in this game, there are tools—spirituality, wisdom, and self-awareness. Whether one believes it or not, life is designed this way, and there is no escape from playing. The only way forward is to understand each flaw and rise above it. That is why we are discussing these weaknesses one by one, placing hesitation at the centre, as it is the root of every major flaw.

Imagine if Duryodhana had controlled his Moha for the throne, the way Bhallaladeva in *Baahubali* could have let go of his greed. Imagine if Hitler had hesitated before massacring the Jews, just as the invaders in India failed to restrain their hunger for destruction. Imagine if people used social media only to connect and express, rather than chasing likes, comments, and subscribers, mistaking virtual validation for self-worth.

Hence, Moha is not just about material things; it is also the attachment to the results of our actions. Every effort we make, every step we take, is often tied to an expectation of success. And when things do not turn out the way we want, frustration takes over. Instead of accepting reality, we look for someone to blame—sometimes it's the weak, the helpless, or society itself. This blame game slowly gives rise to anger, ego, and injustice, making people hesitant to act with fairness and compassion.

At its core, this cycle begins with expectations fuelled by Moha. The deeper the attachment, the greater the disappointment. And when that disappointment turns into anger, it feeds the ego, leading to more suffering. That is why Lord Krishna, in the Bhagavad Gita, reminds us that we have the right to perform our duties, but not to control our outcomes. One should act with sincerity, without being attached to the results, and without falling into inaction.

Freedom is found in the purity of selfless action—when the deed is guided by Dharma and not clouded by the hunger for return.

A society where people act without the burden of Moha, without doubt, and with a pure sense of duty will always move towards justice, equality, and peace. But as long as people remain trapped in attachments, they will continue to struggle with anger, greed, and unrest.

Sage Vishravas, the father of Ravana, was a great ascetic. However, his Moha for power and wealth led him to marry Kaikesi, a woman from the Asura lineage. She desired a son who would rule the three worlds, and Vishravas, being attached to her wishes, agreed. Their union led to the birth of Ravana, Kumbhakarna, and Shurpanakha, who later brought chaos and destruction. Vishravas, though a wise sage, had to witness his own son's downfall because of his Moha to bonding and his wife's ambitions.

Similarly, Thanos, from the *Avengers* series, is attached to his ideology of balancing the universe, believing that wiping out half of existence is the only solution. His deep desire for this belief makes him commit unimaginable destruction without remorse in the movie.

Bhava Santulan is not possible unless one lets go of Moha. However, losing Moha does not mean distributing all wealth or stopping all actions. It simply means learning to share a little, performing one's Kartavya (duty) with Dharma and Satya, and ensuring that no harm befalls others in the process. When a person understands that all human beings are the same, that everyone is connected like a family, life becomes smoother, and everything falls into place naturally.

Nature itself supports those who act with a pure heart. The energies of the universe align with those who carry no greed, no selfish attachments, and no ill intentions. The ones who live with kindness, truth, and selflessness will always find the path ahead illuminated, as if the entire cosmos is helping them move forward. When a person rises above Moha, they do not lose anything, nor do they hesitate in performing good actions. Instead, they gain the true essence of life, peace, harmony, and a sense of oneness with everything around them.

Just as our mobile phone needs regular charging to function, our inner selves also need regular recharging. This renewal comes through Bhava Santulan, which restores balance, clarity, and alignment with Dharma.

Keep in mind, Moha traps, but Bhava Santulan liberates. Moha leads to Adharma, whereas Bhava Santulan aligns with Dharma. The choice is always there—to remain confined in selfishness or to expand into the vastness of life's true purpose.

Exercise

Make a list of ten things that are extremely important in your life—things that hold a significant place in your heart. These could include people, assets, material possessions, power, position, or any living or non-living things that you deeply value.

Now, step into the mindset of Karna, the legendary *daanveer*, known for his unmatched generosity. Imagine that you have to give up three things from your list of ten.

Observe carefully how your mind reacts when you think about letting go of something dear to you. You will undoubtedly notice hesitation, resistance, and a sense of discomfort. This is the mind trapped in Moha, the attachment that makes it difficult to even consider loss in thought.

That doubt, the fear, unwillingness to let go, is your Moha.

The journey beyond Moha begins when you reach a state where losing anything, even yourself, no longer shakes you. Until then, the attachment remains, holding you back from true liberation from Moha and all.

Key Takeaways

Moha is a silent destroyer, binding hearts in endless desires and fears. It traps people in attachments so tightly that they forget how to see beyond themselves. It creates fear of change, fear of loss, and fear of freedom. But through Bhava Santulan, one can rise above this illusion. It teaches that life is not just about clinging, but also about releasing. One who lives in Bhav walks free from Moha and lives fully.

15

SAHAJATA

The Art of Being Simple

सन्तोषः परमं लाभं शान्तिः परमं सुखम्।
सहजं परमं प्रेक्ष्यं धर्मो नास्ति सुखं परम्॥

ONE OF THE MOST VALUABLE LESSONS FROM ALMOST ALL THE Upanishads explains that contentment is the greatest wealth, and inner peace is the highest happiness. Sahajata (simplicity) is the ultimate virtue, for there is no greater joy than living in harmony with one's natural self and Dharma.

Sahajata means simplicity. It is the state of being natural, pure, and untouched by artificial layers. It reflects what is original, unforced, and effortless. Sahajata is not about being ordinary, but about being real. It is the quiet strength of truth, where nothing is added and nothing is hidden. In Sahajata, there is no need to impress, no urge to perform, and no fear of judgement. It is the essence of being rooted in our true nature. When a person lives with Sahajata, their thoughts are clear, their actions are honest, and their presence feels peaceful.

Yet, human beings often struggle to accept things as they naturally are. Since the beginning of civilisation, there has been a constant urge to modify, control, and reshape everything around us. This tendency extends not only to the external world but also to our inner selves. We try to change the laws of nature to suit our comfort, adjust our behaviour to meet social expectations, alter our ideologies to gain approval, and even modify our food habits, appearance, and surroundings to match imagined standards. From taming wild animals to redesigning the human face, from unnatural routines to forced lifestyles, we continue to drift away from Sahajata. What is simple and natural is often seen as incomplete or boring.

In our constant pursuit of progress, we often overlook the quiet beauty of what exists. True peace begins when we stop forcing change and start accepting the truth of nature, both outside and within.

Instead of embracing the beauty of what already exists, we chase after what we believe should exist. We refine, redefine, and reconstruct things, thinking that by altering the original, we are making it better. But in doing so, we often move further away from the natural flow of life.

Some changes and alterations are truly beneficial and deserve admiration, as they contribute to the well-being of society and improve people's lives. However, not everything can be justified under the goodness of a few changes.

Simplicity is not a sign of weakness, but a quiet power held deep within.

Doubts play their role here as well. It stops people from embracing Sahajata and being their true selves. It makes them afraid to show their natural form, fearing that they may not be accepted as they are. So, instead of living in their simplicity, people start imitating others, thinking that by doing so, they will gain more attention and recognition.

In this Kalpana (illusion), they believe that those who dress stylishly, speak impressively, or behave in a certain way hold more value than they do. Without even questioning this belief, they change themselves, unknowingly losing their natural essence. They become a shadow of someone else, thinking they are improving, but in reality, they are just moving further away from their true self.

The same happens with today's youth in large numbers, when they fail to recognise their natural talent and inner strengths. Instead of identifying their core competency, which is the ability to do something with ease and excellence in a way that feels natural, they begin to imitate others. They follow the footsteps of those who are already successful, thinking that copying their style, habits, or choices will bring the same results. But in doing so, they move away from their true potential. What they forget is that success is not a formula to repeat but a truth to realise. Every individual is born with a unique ability, a natural flow that leads to growth when nurtured sincerely. Imitation only creates doubts, and in the end, they neither reach great heights nor do justice to their flair. Real achievement begins when one walks the path of Sahajata, the way of natural strength and honest self-expression.

Imagine Virat Kohli trying to imitate Neeraj Chopra and Neeraj imitating Virat. It would make no sense. Both are legends because they recognised their natural abilities and honed them. Those who understand their true strengths and nurture them find real success, while those who imitate others eventually fade away, lost in time and failure.

That is why Sahajata is essential at every stage of life. Being Sahaj means being natural and real. When a person stays true to their authentic self, it enhances their personality, their way of living, and most importantly, their peace of mind. There is no need to impress others by changing something unnecessarily. True power comes from accepting oneself as they are, without doubt, without pretending.

Pretending is perhaps the finest form of acting and, for that, it deserves nothing less than an Oscar.

It is ironic that people openly copy someone but refuse to accept it. To address it more gracefully, some call it 'having a role model' or 'drawing inspiration'. But if you look closely, what they are really doing is trying to become someone else, whether in a big or a small way. They dress like them, talk like them, think like them, and even shape their dreams to match. It may sound impressive at first, but ultimately, it is an imitation and a copy. Regardless of how polished it may be, it can never possess the strength of originality. It lacks soul.

Sahajata applies to every aspect of life. How we work, how we live, maintain relationships, and conduct business or do a job. Simplicity is not just a virtue; it is the best approach to life. Those who embrace Sahajata in their work and trade rise to greatness, just like Ratan Tata, whose simplicity in leadership and vision made him a giant in the corporate world. Those who live with Sahajata in their daily lives reflect the grace of Lord Ram, whose righteousness and simplicity made him the ideal king. And those who remain unaffected by name, fame, and popularity, yet stay grounded in Sahajata, become like Rajinikanth, a South superstar who remains humble despite his immense success.

Life is simple, yet we complicate it, drawn by our strange habit of creating our own troubles.

Ghatotkacha, the son of Bhima, also lives by his natural strength. He arrives when needed, fights with full force, and sacrifices himself without asking for anything. His actions flow from his loyalty and Dharma, not from pride or desire.

In the Ramayana, Shabari, the old tribal woman, is a pure example of Sahajata. She lives alone in the forest, waiting patiently for Lord Ram, without any demand or condition. Her devotion is natural. She does not follow any royal tradition, yet her simplicity touches divinity. She does not try to be great, but her innocence becomes sacred.

Every individual has a pre-written life filled with success, wealth, health, and a defined lifespan. Yet, instead of flowing with it, people try to forcefully reshape it beyond what is meant for them, believing that they must become the greatest, the most successful, or the most admired. It is not about lacking ambition; rather, it is about being impractical in chasing something that is not aligned with their natural path.

The wounds of life find healing in acceptance, yet only when it is whole and without condition.

Sahajata teaches the first and most important lesson—acceptance is natural, and within acceptance lies true peace. Life does not demand struggle; it simply asks for acceptance. No matter how harsh or comfortable one's life journey is, the person who accepts life and Dharma as it is lives with joy and full awareness. But instead of embracing this Sahajata, we push ourselves into the endless race of proving ourselves to society. We compare, we compete, and when we fall short, we feel embarrassed and depressed.

We are the ones who nurture ego, greed, and endless desires, and then act upon them in ways that often go against Dharma. Yet, we expect life to remain simple, peaceful, and in our favour. How can that be possible? When we walk away from the path of balance, we invite imbalance. We create complications with our own choices and decisions and then expect life to offer us quick and magical solutions. We ignore the laws of nature, disturb the harmony of body and mind, and then hope for sudden relief when disease arrives. But life does not work that way. It reflects what we give it—the actions we take, the thoughts we carry, and the intentions we set all return to us in some form. If we want peace, we must first live peacefully. If we wish for healing, we must first stop harming. Life is not a puzzle to solve but a mirror to reflect.

Exercise

Write the dishonest answers as 'Yes' or 'No' to see how many 'Yes' and 'No' you have received.

- Are you truly a kind human being?
- Is your mind in your control?
- Do you live to eat?
- Is anger your companion?
- Do you hate those who hate you?
- Do you hesitate to say no?
- Does your appearance make you feel weak?
- Have you ever tried to steal something?
- Do you remember the names of people?
- Are you breathing now?

Now, you might have expected that I would ask you to write honest answers, but instead, I asked for dishonest answers.

This turned a simple exercise into a complicated one, as you had to read carefully and think twice before responding to such straightforward questions.

Still, if you have more yeses, then it's time to work on yourself to become more Sahaj (simple and natural). If you have more nos, then you are already on the path of Sahajata. Keep going!

Key Takeaways

This chapter emphasises that simplicity (Sahajata) leads to success, while complication and blind imitation result in failure. It highlights how individuals who embrace simplicity, authenticity, and clarity achieve greatness, while those who overcomplicate life or try to imitate others struggle and fade away. By following Sahajata, one can achieve peace, clarity, Dharma and long-term success, while those who complicate life with unnecessary desires and imitation ultimately fail.

16

Shanti over Chanchalta

Overcoming Restlessness

चञ्चलं हि मनः कृष्ण प्रमाथि बलवद् दृढम्।
तस्याहं निग्रहं मन्ये वायोरिव सुदुष्करम्॥

One of the most valuable lessons from the Bhagavad Gita (6.34), this shloka explains that the nature of the mind is Chanchal (restless), always wandering between desires, worries, and distractions. Just as it is impossible to hold the wind in one's hand, it is equally challenging to control an unsettled mind. However, through meditation, self-discipline, and devotion, one can gradually bring stability and experience inner peace (Shanti).

If someone ever tries to write a book on how and why the human mind is so restless and unstable, or Chanchal, it will likely become the longest book ever written on this planet. The reasons behind our mental instability are endless, as countless as the stars scattered across the galaxy. A single thought, a forgotten Smriti, a missed opportunity, an imagined fear, or even a small word spoken by someone can disturb the peace of the mind. Desires, comparisons, expectations, regrets, and doubts keep the mind spinning like a wheel that never stops. The mind moves in many directions at once, rarely staying still. Its restlessness is not the fault of the world, but the result of how we respond to it. Understanding this is the first step towards Shanti (peace).

Thus, the fastest thing in the world is not light, not sound, but the speed at which a person loses their mental stability through fearful or doubtful thoughts. Just hearing certain words like loss, failure, accident, death, darkness, police, hospital, court, or rejection can shake one's inner balance within seconds. Even simple everyday words like get out, can't, won't, or don't are enough to make the heart race, the mind panic, and the body stiffen.

This is what true restlessness feels like, not caused by the world but created within by how we react to it. Yet, despite knowing this, we continue searching for peace outside. We try to buy it, earn it, chase it, or expect it from others, forgetting that peace is not something to be found. It is something to be experienced within.

Peace doesn't arise from merely closing the eyes and taking deep breaths; it blossoms only when the restlessness of the mind is truly stilled.

We carry so much fear, doubts, and worries that even the mere sound of negativity shakes us. This is the very nature of Chanchalta—an unstable mind jumps from one fear to another, one worry to another, never resting in peace. Unless we learn to anchor ourselves in truth, acceptance, surrender, Dharma, and avoidance, this instability will never stop chasing us.

A restless individual is always in a hurry, impatient, and often makes decisions that they later regret. On the other hand, a calm-minded person remains focused and steady, choosing silence over unnecessary reactions. Restlessness clouds a person's vision, limiting their perception and filling their mind with duality, doubts, and complications. This is one of the biggest struggles people face today, whether in personal or professional life. No amount of money can buy a single moment of true peace; it can only be achieved through patience, calmness, and consistency in avoiding unnecessary restlessness.

The echoes of consistency can be heard in the life of Saint Dnyaneshwar, the divine prodigy from Maharashtra. Orphaned at a young age, with only his three brothers and a sister as his world, he could have surrendered to the pain of loss. Instead, he chose perseverance. With a heart full of devotion and a mind burning with knowledge, he took it upon himself the monumental task of translating the Bhagavad Gita into Marathi, a language the common people could understand. He did this at the mere age of sixteen.

This is the undeniable truth of life: Those who stand unwavering in their pursuit, who entertain no doubt, who seek no shortcuts, are the ones who attain both greatness and peace.

But doubt is the poison that spoils everything. The moment a person starts doubting their journey, they derail themselves from success and become restless. Hesitation makes people compare effort with outcome, and when they believe the effort is too great, they abandon their dreams and aspirations, looking for something easier. But what great achievement has ever come from choosing the easy and shortcut path?

The most powerful force in the entire universe that can make you fall is your own self-doubt.

One of my friends has unknowingly become a living example of inconsistency and fearful living. His life moves in circles, not with growth but with unfinished starts and silent retreats. He begins things with great energy, filled with hope and excitement, but leaves them midway with a pocketful of excuses. He hates his job deeply, yet he continues to stay in it. Every month, frustration builds up, and he carefully types out a resignation letter. He reads it again and again, imagining the proud moment he will walk out free. But when it is time to send it, doubt steps in and the letter is quietly deleted.

At work, he enters meetings with full interest, notebook in hand, nodding to every word. But within minutes, his hand slides under the table, unlocking his phone, scrolling through social media while the meeting moves on without him. The dream of becoming an entrepreneur also visits him regularly. A new idea excites him every few weeks. He gathers friends, builds plans, starts a WhatsApp group, and talks with passion. But as the time to act arrives, the excitement fades, the group becomes silent, and the idea is replaced by a new one next month. For him, it is a cycle of loud beginnings and quiet disappearances.

He has countless fears that come in strange shapes. He fears a dent in his car, so he avoids driving. He fears his phone breaking, so he wraps it in heavy protection. He fears financial loss, so he becomes overly cautious. He fears public embarrassment, so he avoids conversations. He fears losing status, so he constantly pretends to be happy and successful, even when he feels lost inside. This collection of fears and hesitation keeps him restless, both in thought and action.

Still, he regularly joins meditation classes, visits spiritual retreats, and buys books that promise 'peace of mind'. Yet, real Shanti stays far from him, as far as the distance between the sun and the earth. Because peace does not come from doing more, but from facing the self honestly. Until the fears are recognised and the hesitation is addressed, no book or programme can offer what only inner courage can bring.

However, in today's fast-paced world, there are countless ways to fall into the trap of Chanchalta. Distractions from consistency make it difficult to stay stable and focused.

Even great warriors and divine beings faced moments of restlessness, but they overcame them through wisdom and guidance. When Arjun hesitated on the battlefield, he became restless, unsure of his duty. But instead of staying in doubt, he sought wise guidance from Lord Krishna and found clarity.

Hanuman, once cursed in childhood, forgot his true strength. When the time came to leap across the ocean, he doubted, thinking he was powerless. But through the wise consultation of Jambavan, he remembered his abilities and accomplished the impossible.

These examples show that wise guidance during moments of restlessness can lead to stability, greatness, and alignment with Dharma.

A restless person is not only harmful to themselves but to society as well. Scriptures have shown how Duryodhana, Ravana, Jarasandha, Bhasmasura, and Lavanasura, all consumed by Chanchalta, brought destruction upon themselves and the whole society.

People today are desperately searching for ways to escape their restlessness, yet they don't even know what they are truly looking for. They seek stability in addictions, desires, motivational workshops, and retreats, hoping to find peace. But despite all their efforts, the restlessness remains.

Why so?

Because they have become habituated to being restless. They have unknowingly become slaves to Chanchalta, constantly chasing peace yet never finding it.

The search for peace is the most foolish one ever, for how can one seek what was never truly lost?

One of my acquaintances is a perfect example of restlessness. He gets restless the moment his mobile battery drops below 20 per cent, running around looking for a charger as if his life depends on it. Whenever he sends a message, he expects an instant reply, and if the other person takes time to respond, he starts overthinking and becomes even more restless.

If the Wi-Fi stops working, it's as if civilisation has collapsed. If his online food order takes time, he calls customer care and the delivery guy repeatedly, demanding updates. If the TV remote is not in its usual place, he declares an emergency at home and makes everyone search for it.

Even in situations where he has no control, like traffic jams or a slow-moving elevator, he still becomes restless, unable to wait and accept things as they are.

One day, he came to me for advice, and I told him to calm down and accept things as they happen.

A week later, he met me again and said, 'I spent hours thinking and making plans on how not to be restless about these things . . . but then, new things happened that made me restless!'

I asked him about those new things. He sighed and gave me another list: 'I forgot my password and spent two hours trying to recall it', 'The barber cut my hair too short the last time, and I kept feeling embarrassed about it, thinking why the hair growth is so slow', 'I was in a queue, and the line next to me was moving faster. It made me restless again', 'And you were typing something on the messaging app, and then you stopped. I kept thinking, what were you going to say? So, I got restless!'

I smiled and said, 'See? We have become so used to restlessness that when nothing makes us restless, we become restless about that, too.'

This is the real problem. We have made restlessness our normal state, and peace feels like a strange visitor. We search for silence outside but carry noise within. We chase peace like it is lost somewhere far, while it patiently waits inside us.

In truth, peace is not something to be found or created. It is always present, calm, and steady, like the sky behind passing clouds. We just need to stop feeding the storm of thoughts and allow peace to settle naturally. It does not require effort, only acceptance. When we stop disturbing the stillness with fear, overthinking, and endless doubts, peace rises on its own, just like a calm lake reflects the sky when the wind stops. Peace is not missing; we just need to stop pushing it away.

Shanti is not just a word; it is an experiential state, a rare jewel of Dharma where all worries, regrets, and tensions dissolve into stillness. It is a state where the mind rests, the heart breathes freely, and consciousness awakens. In this sacred space, one does not just live but truly experiences life with a deep awareness of every breath, every moment, and the aliveness of the soul.

Just as two lions cannot rule over the same pride, Shanti and Chanchalta cannot exist together. One must leave for the other to stay. If restlessness controls our mind, peace will slip away like sand through our fingers. But if peace takes its rightful place, restlessness will vanish like mist in the morning sun.

Restlessness is not just about running around physically; it is present in our thoughts, emotions, habits, attitudes, and reactions. It makes us jump from one thing to another, seeking, wanting, desiring, craving, never satisfied, always hesitant, always hungry for more.

This is why people struggle so much in life, as they unknowingly search for peace while tightly holding onto restlessness.

Keeping doubts within while seeking inner peace is like fire trying to burn the ocean. Remember, no one is born perfect; it is their choices that carve their greatness.

So, does life offer choices?

Heaven and hell are not places far away; they exist within us, in our experiences. If we choose Chanchalta, we live in our own created hell, always anxious, always seeking, never content. Whereas, if we choose Shanti, we create our own heaven, where nothing shakes us, nothing disturbs us, nothing makes us hesitant, and we flow with life like a calm river.

So, the decision is simple. Do we choose peace or chaos? Do we choose heaven or hell?

'Ashant mann' (restless mind) cannot create anything apart from chaos, struggle, and impatience within. Whereas a calm and focused mind can create miracles.

When Albert Einstein was asked about his secret to brilliant ideas, he said that the monotony and solitude of a quiet life stimulate the creative mind. Einstein did not rush through life. He spent hours in deep thought, allowing ideas to naturally flow, rather than forcing them. This is the power of a calm mind—it does not chase ideas, it attracts them.

Similarly, Nikola Tesla, the legendary inventor, once said that the mind is sharper and keener in seclusion and uninterrupted solitude. Originality thrives in silence.

Always remember one simple truth: The more we chase, the more we fear. The more we compare, the more we hesitate. The more we doubt, the more we hold on to our ego. The more we desire, the more we create inner struggle. The more we live in Smriti, holding on to the past, the more we allow Maya to blind us. And in this restless state, no matter how much we achieve—money, property, position, or fame—real joy remains distant. True bliss does not live in noise. It lives in the quiet stillness of a peaceful mind. That is the real Shanti, the calm state of the awakened self, the true state of Shiva within. The true form of Dharma lies within.

The mind that lives in constant motion trembles when it meets stillness.

A Chanchal mind is a breeding ground for restlessness and disease. But a mind in Shanti becomes a heaven for health, clarity, and higher consciousness. A research study by Danah Henriksen, Carmen Richardson, and Kyle Shack, published in the international journal Thinking Skills and Creativity, highlights that mindfulness practices, often understood as a way to overcome mental restlessness, nurture essential skills and habits of mind. Such habits not only strengthen creative thinking but also cultivate a mind that is steady, calm, and receptive to fresh ideas and perspectives. Focus is not possible where the mind keeps running. It is born when the mind learns to stay still.

So, choose wisely. Life is not forever. It is a precious gift that lives only in the present moment. And these moments are not waiting. They are rushing forward like a bullet train. If you keep thinking, keep doubting, keep planning without living, the train will pass. Before it leaves, catch it. Sit down peacefully. Look out of the window. And enjoy the journey, not as a passenger full of fear, but as a soul in Apurva Shanti.

That is where real life begins.

Exercise

The simplest yet most challenging exercise mentioned in this book so far is as follows:

Find a quiet, isolated place where you can be completely undisturbed for ten minutes. Ensure that the surroundings are silent, free from crowds, and that no one—neither your mobile phone nor any individual—interrupts you.

Sit comfortably, relax your body, and calm your mind. With a pen and diary in hand, keenly observe each thought that arises in your mind. You may choose to write them down.

For these ten minutes, simply note down every thought that enters your mind while maintaining a state of quiet observation. Try to remain as calm and composed as possible.

After the time is up, review your thoughts. You will likely notice that most of them revolve around imagination, fear, future planning, irrelevant matters, or memories of past regrets and pleasures.

Interestingly, you will realise that none of these thoughts are truly relevant to the present moment in which you are evaluating yourself.

Through this exercise, you will understand how your mind becomes an obstacle in experiencing even ten minutes of true peace (Shanti). It constantly distracts you with an influx of thoughts (Chanchalta), making you restless and compelling you to chase after them.

Practise this exercise daily to gradually train your mind and detach from unnecessary thoughts. Over time, you will develop better control over your mental clutter, allowing you to experience deeper moments of stillness, clarity, and inner peace.

Key Takeaways

Shanti is priceless, while Chanchalta is a quiet curse. These two states of mind shape life in diverse ways. Shanti brings clarity, calmness, and deep contentment. It allows the mind to think clearly, act wisely, and stay balanced. Chanchalta steals that peace, filling the mind with doubt, distraction, and confusion. A restless mind keeps wandering, unable to focus or feel joy. Where there is Shanti, there is strength and Dharma. Where there is Chanchalta, there is struggle.

17

SANKALP SHAKTI

Firm Determination Assures Winning

यज्जाग्रतो दूरमुदैति दैवं तदु सुप्तस्य तथैवैति।
दूरङ्गमं ज्योतिषां ज्योतिरेकं तन्मे मनः शिवसङ्कल्पमस्तु॥

ONE OF THE MOST VALUABLE SHLOKAS, THIS IS FROM THE Shiva Sankalpa Sukta, which appears in the Yajurveda (34.1). The text describes the divine force of the mind, which has the ability to travel great distances both when awake and during sleep. This mind is depicted as a far-reaching entity and the source of all illumination—a supreme light. May that mind be filled with pure and auspicious intentions (Shiva Sankalpa).

Sankalpa is not just a thought or a fleeting wish; it is a profound and unwavering resolve. It is the firm decision of the mind that no obstacle can weaken. Sankalpa (Commitment) gives direction to energy, turns dreams into actions, and transforms the impossible into achievable. It is the quiet force behind every meaningful success. Similarly, Shakti (inner strength) is not just raw power, but the strength that rises from inner determination. True Shakti is the will to stay committed to one's path, to stand firm in truth, and to move forward with clarity and courage. When Sankalpa and Shakti unite, they become the foundation of transformation.

Nothing is more shameful than holding a Sankalp within, only to let it be buried in the graveyard of hundreds of forgotten Sankalpas.

In the Mahabharata, Bhishma Pratigya (Bhishma's Vow) is one of the greatest examples of Sankalpa—firm determination that remained unbroken till his last breath. It is a perfect demonstration of how unshakeable Sankalpa can define character and inspire generations.

Every year, on December 31st or January 1st, millions of people around the world make new resolutions. They promise themselves they will wake up early, exercise daily, eat healthily, work with more focus, or bring some positive change to their habits. These promises are not just casual thoughts; they are expressions of Sankalpa Shakti, the inner power of commitment towards self-improvement.

Now, pause for a moment and reflect. How many such resolutions have you taken in your life so far? The number is probably countless. And now ask yourself, how many of them have you truly followed through and fulfilled? The answer, for most, is very few, sometimes none at all.

Why does this Adharma happen? The answer is simple. Most resolutions are taken without true Sankalpa (Commitment). They are born from temporary excitement, emotional pressure, or social influence. They lack depth, clarity, and staying power. A mind filled with hesitation, self-doubt, or fear of difficulty will never reach the goal. But the one who takes a Sankalpa with full determination, and stands by it without looking back, is the one who achieves lasting success in both personal and professional life. True Sankalpa is not a momentary thought; it is a decision that becomes a path.

Those who took strong Sankalpa (commitment) changed the world. It was Rama's Sankalpa (intent) to end the evil rule of Ravana and establish dharma. It was Lord Krishna's Sankalpa (pledge) to uphold righteousness and guide humanity. It was Hanuman's Sankalpa (aspiration) to serve Lord Ram with unwavering devotion without ever thinking of himself. It was Nachiketa's Sankalpa Shakti to understand the truth of death and immortality, which made him fearless even in front of Yama, the Lord of Death. It was Dhruva's Sankalpa that led him to perform such intense penance that he attained an immortal place in the sky as the Dhruva Nakshatra (Pole Star). It was Satyavrat's Sankalpa (aim) that ensured the knowledge of the Vedas was preserved during the great flood, allowing civilisation to rise again.

Even in modern India, history has been shaped by those who took Sankalpa and stayed committed to it. It was Mahatma Gandhi's Sankalpa to free India through Ahimsa (non-violence), which led other freedom fighters to the end of British rule. It was Dr B. R. Ambedkar's Sankalpa to give India a just and equal constitution, ensuring democracy for generations to come. It was Dr A. P. J. Abdul Kalam's Sankalpa to make India self-reliant in science and technology, which turned India into a space and defence power. It was Sardar Vallabhbhai Patel's Sankalpa to unite 562 princely states into one strong nation, ensuring India remained one country. It was J. R. D. Tata's Sankalpa that made India an industrial powerhouse, setting the foundation for future economic growth.

Sankalpa is such a powerful force that even those who walked the path of darkness and destruction used it to their advantage. Ravana made a Sankalpa to abduct Sita, fully aware of the consequences, yet he moved forward with complete determination. Duryodhana's Sankalpa was to destroy the

Pandavas, and he pursued it with unwavering focus, despite all warnings. Kansa's Sankalpa was to kill Lord Krishna even before his birth, and he lived every moment of his life with that goal in mind. Hiranyakashipu made a Sankalpa to kill his son, Prahlada, simply because the child worshipped Lord Vishnu. But in the end, his ego and arrogance were crushed by Lord Narasimha. These examples portray that Sankalpa, whether used for Dharma or Adharma, holds immense power. What matters is not just the strength of one's determination, but the direction in which it is applied with the inner Shakti and wisdom.

Sankalpa works both ways—it can uplift a soul to greatness or lead to complete destruction, all depending on how it is held and honoured.

A committed Sankalpa, when based on truth, Dharma, and service to society, can create miracles. But a Sankalpa driven by ego, selfishness, and destruction can lead to ruin.

Modern psychology, too, supports the power of Sankalpa (determination). Neuroscience research states that when a person makes a firm resolution, it creates new neural pathways in the brain, reinforcing focus, discipline, and resilience. This is why individuals with strong determination are more likely to succeed despite challenges. Scientific studies prove that dopamine (the motivation chemical) increases when people commit to a goal with strong conviction. This means that Sankalpa not only influences the mind but also alters brain chemistry, making success more achievable. As noted in a review from the Consulting Psychology Journal and as highlighted by the National Institutes of Health (NIH).

The difference between an extraordinary life and an ordinary one lies in Sankalpa. A person who takes a decision with firm conviction, who commits with full heart and unwavering focus, and who does not allow doubt to disturb the mind, is the one who rises towards greatness. Such a person moves forward with clarity, even when the path is difficult.

On the other hand, the one who keeps doubting, who questions their own abilities, and who delays action repeatedly, remains stuck. They watch others move ahead, while their dreams slowly fade into regret. Sankalpa is not just about desire; it is about commitment without turning back.

Take a moment and think about the people you admire the most. It could be a leader, a business tycoon, a spiritual master, a scientist, or even someone from your own family. What makes them different from you? Is it intelligence? Is it luck? Is it wealth? No. The one thing that truly separates them from others is their unshakeable determination, their commitment to their goal, and their ability to take a firm Sankalpa and never waver from it.

Now, take this one word, Sankalpa Shakti, out of their lives and try to imagine their journey without it.

Commitment is not merely a resolution of words; it is a sacred responsibility to be carried with honour until it is fulfilled.

A scientist would have abandoned their experiments after the first failure. The leader would have given up after the first challenge. The businessman would have hesitated at the risk. The spiritual master would have doubted the inner path. The warrior would have feared the battle.

Without Sankalpa, none of them would have achieved anything remarkable. And if they had hesitated instead of moving forward with conviction, they would have been lost in the crowd of ordinary people, just like so many of us who never fulfil their true potential.

If the only difference between you and them is Sankalpa, then what is stopping you from achieving the same level of success?

It is self-doubt.

Where they chose to take a firm decision and stay committed to it, most people hesitate, overthink, doubt, and step back. This hesitation, this self-doubt, this constant analysing of actions is what separates extraordinary people from ordinary ones.

We have read countless stories of determination and consistency. We have heard motivational speeches, watched inspiring movies, and listened to success stories over and over again. Yet, most people still struggle to take action in their own lives. The reason is simple—the mind is bored of these words because it only listens but never implements. If we truly understood and applied the power of determination, we wouldn't need to be reminded of it again and again. However, the fact that it is missing from our lives proves that we have only read about it, not lived it.

Can a child be born in the fifth month of pregnancy? No, nature follows its course, and patience is the key. In the same way, success follows consistency—there are no shortcuts, no premature victories. Those who hesitate, who give up at the first sign of difficulty, are like people who dream of becoming inventors but only have the patience to change a lightbulb, not to create one.

Let's look at a simple truth.

If someone asks: Do you want more money? Do you want a promotion? Do you want to eat your favourite food? Do you want to take more rest? We immediately smile and say, yes, without doubt. We have heard these questions a thousand times before, but we still like hearing them because they give us pleasure. But when it comes to something meaningful, when someone says, take a Sankalpa, commit to your goal, or have firm determination, most people simply avoid it. Because deep inside, they have surrendered themselves to hesitation.

But the real problem is that they don't accept it. They still consider themselves warriors of life, thinking they are fighting every day, making efforts, struggling, and moving forward. But the reality is, they are hiding their true power, Sankalpa and taking shelter under doubt, which is nothing but the friend of failure. And if someone keeps standing on the side of hesitation while pretending to fight in the battle of life, how can they ever win?

The truth is, no one can win until they choose the right side.

You have to take a strong Sankalpa, commit to it fully, and never look back. You must decide whether you want to create an extraordinary life that inspires others or become one of those who fade away in the ashes of time because they kept doubting, waiting, and postponing their actions.

In the Mahabharata, the story of Lord Parshurama, an avatar of Lord Vishnu, stands as a powerful example of the strength of Sankalpa.

When his father was killed by King Kartavirya Arjun, Parshurama took a mighty pledge to destroy all corrupt and arrogant Kshatriyas who had misused their power and turned away from Dharma. His Sankalpa was not driven by anger alone, but by a deep commitment to restore balance and righteousness. With firm resolve and unmatched focus, he single-handedly defeated twenty-one generations of unethical Kshatriya kings.

This story reminds us that when Sankalpa is pure, unshakable, and aligned with Dharma, even what seems impossible can be achieved.

Exercise

Create a simple table with three columns. In the first column, write the heading 'Aspiration'. In the second column, write 'Sankalpa' (Firm Determination). In the third column, write 'Hesitation' (Excuses and Barriers).

Now, list your top five aspirations, dreams, and ambitions in life. These should be the goals that truly matter to you, the ones that define your success and fulfilment.

Against each aspiration, write in the Sankalpa column: 'What Sankalpa must I take to achieve it?' And in the hesitation column, write: 'What kind of hesitation and excuses will stop me from achieving it?'

While writing, do not try to protect your self-image or convince yourself that you are already on the right path. This activity is not for others; it is for you alone. No one will judge you except yourself. The more honest you are, the clearer your path to success will become.

Once you have completed this reflection, analyse your answers carefully. This simple exercise will give you a clear picture of what you want, what you must do, and what may stand in your way.

Now, focus on the third column, the hesitation and excuses. Acknowledge that these are the only things preventing your success. Make a firm decision to eliminate them, strengthen your Sankalpa Shakti, and commit to action.

My best wishes are with you. May you remove hesitation, act with unwavering determination, and achieve all five of your aspirations in the coming years.

Key Takeaways

Sankalpa Shakti is the force of firm determination that transforms thought into action and dreams into reality. It stands directly against hesitation, which is the biggest barrier to success. Every great achievement begins with an unwavering decision, not endless thinking. Hesitation breeds doubt, confusion, and fear, keeping us stuck in the cycle of overthinking. We delay action, waiting for the perfect moment, only to find it has passed and left us with regret. Sankalpa is not about bold words but quiet Shakti. It is the inner voice that says: 'I will move ahead no matter what'. With Sankalpa Shakti, even the impossible becomes possible, Adharma becomes Dharma.

18

Kala Is Sacred

Respecting Every Moment

काल एव पुरस्तात्काल एवान्ततः।

One of the most valuable shlokas from the Maitrayaniya Upanishad (6.15), this verse underscores the omnipresence of Kala (time), emphasising that time encompasses and influences every aspect of existence. It serves as a reminder of the transient nature of life and the universe, urging individuals to recognise the significance of time in their spiritual and worldly pursuits.

Someone once said, 'Time stays long enough for those who use it wisely.' This simple line holds deep truth—time is not about how much we have, but how meaningfully we live each moment.

Kala, or time, is not just a measure of days, hours, or passing moments. It is the very essence of life. Every second that moves forward carries the unseen energy of existence. It is the breath of the universe, the quiet rhythm guiding every action, choice, and change. When we waste time, we are not merely losing minutes, we are losing a part of our life.

Time does not favour anyone. It gives equal opportunity to all. Whether rich or poor, powerful or powerless, known or unknown, everyone receives the same twenty-four hours in a day. Yet what separates the achievers from the dreamers is not how much time they have, but how they use it. Kala is the silent witness to every effort, every delay, every excuse, and every breakthrough. It is the invisible force behind every story of transformation.

Unlike fate, wealth, privilege, status, or karma, time is the only asset that is distributed equally. It does not judge by age, caste, gender, status, or birthplace. It is the most democratic gift, yet the most ignored. While some use it to build empires of knowledge, skill, and character, others let it pass in distractions, complaints, doubts or indecision.

The wise treat time as a sacred resource. They take action while others wait. They create while others hesitate. They turn their thoughts into plans, and their plans into reality. Those who fail to value time often realise its worth only when it has slipped through their hands. Kala teaches without speaking and punishes without warning.

In this fleeting moment, you are the oldest you have ever been and the youngest you will ever be, a breath suspended between was and will be.

Time goes unnoticed when abundant yet becomes priceless when it's about to slip away.

Time is not just the ticking of the clock. It is the silent medium through which all creation takes shape. Every idea, every change, every success begins within the frame of time. It is through time that we learn, grow, heal, and evolve. To honour time is to honour life. And to misuse it is to invite regret.

Use it wisely, for Kala does not stop. It moves forward, whether we act or not. In the end, it is not how much time we had, but how consciously we lived it that defines the story of our life.

Every great invention, every monumental achievement, and every act of greatness was made possible only because someone used their time wisely. With time, we can plan, execute, and refine our strategies. It allows us to set goals, allocate resources, and progress steadily towards success. In its purest sense, time is the currency of creation. A force that, when used wisely, turns thoughts and ambitions into actual outcomes.

It is from this deep realisation that the concept of time management emerged. The world recognised that without properly utilising time, even the most brilliant ideas would remain unfulfilled. However, hesitation often becomes the greatest obstacle to time utilisation.

People hesitate to step out of their comfort zones, avoid taking action, and delay essential decisions within time. Doubts breed regret, for time once lost can never be reclaimed. Despite the knowledge that time is irreplaceable, many fail to honour its significance.

Since the very first footsteps of humankind on this earth, one deep illusion has always walked beside us: The belief that we have enough time. We live as if the sun will rise for us a thousand more times, as if we have been promised tomorrows. But the truth is, no one knows how many breaths remain, how many sunrises are yet to see. What we hold now is this one breath, this one moment, alive, precious, slipping silently into the past even as we speak. Yet, so many of us waste this sacred gift in endless thinking, caught in mental loops of what-ifs, should-haves, and could-bes. We forget we are not machines made to think endlessly; we are life itself, made to live, to feel the wind, to laugh deeply, to love fully, and to be present in the now with all our being.

Many think that death is a faraway event, something that visits others, not them, and not so soon. They believe Kala is like a river that flows forever, an ocean with no shore. So, they float through life, wasting days scrolling through screens, chasing temporary thrills, escaping the silence where life whispers truth. This dangerous lie that time is plenty has fooled generations. It has lulled humanity into a sleepwalk, delaying dreams, postponing generosity and kindness, pushing away the things that matter with a simple thought: I will do it later. But later is a myth.

This is the reason why, despite a global population of over eight hundred crores, only a few thousand truly live a life of wealth, achievement, wisdom, and success. The rest? They are simply passing time, caught in the loop of temporary pleasures, stuck to their smart gadgets, scrolling endlessly, and consuming information that does not serve them. They have forgotten that time is not something to 'pass'; it is something to utilise and cherish.

We only understand the importance of time when we are forced into situations that remind us of its fleeting nature. It happens when we rush to catch a train and realise we are late, when we run to the exam hall with just minutes left, when we are stuck in traffic while an important meeting awaits, or when we miss the first few scenes of a movie because we were delayed. These moments bring a sudden panic and urgency, but they last only for a short while.

The realisation fades quickly, and soon, we return to our usual ways, wasting hours without thought, postponing our goals, and assuming there will always be another day.

This understanding of time rarely crosses our minds in daily life. We don't think about it until, one day, we look into the mirror and see wrinkles on our faces. Even then, instead of reflecting on where all the time went, instead of realising that life is moving faster than we imagined, we start looking for solutions to reduce wrinkles. The real problem is not ageing; it is the unnoticed loss of time.

Time blesses the mindful with the present moment; it curses the careless with only memories and dreams.

Time is the most precious gift given to us, and how we use it shapes our life and the world around us. Few have understood the value of time like Adi Shankaracharya, the great saint who walked across India with a mission much bigger than himself. At an age when most children are just beginning to learn about life, he had already set out on his journey. He knew that time should not be wasted in useless things but used for a higher purpose. He dedicated every moment to uniting people, reviving Dharma, and bringing back the wisdom of Sanatan philosophy. He used his time wisely to write powerful scriptures, like Vivekachudamani, which is still a guiding light for those who seek truth, wisdom, and Dharma.

Among those who understand time and use it wisely is Maharishi Vyasa, the revered author of the Mahabharata. He understood Dharma deeply. Through his teachings, he emphasised that Kala is inseparable from karma and destiny. Everything happens when it is meant to happen, not before and not after. It is not enough to simply desire something; one must act at the right moment. Just as a seed cannot grow into a tree before its time, life unfolds only when karma and time align.

Bhishma, one of the greatest warriors and statesmen of the Mahabharata, had a profound understanding of time. He was given the power to choose the moment of his death, and he used this gift wisely. Lying on a bed of arrows after the great war of Kurukshetra, he waited for Uttarayana, the sacred period when the sun moves northward, before leaving his mortal body. His decision was not just about personal salvation; it was a testament to how one can align their actions with the flow of time to achieve the best outcome.

Chanakya, the great strategist and philosopher, also recognised the power of Kala. He did not waste a single moment in idleness but used time to shape history. It was through his vision and timely action that the Maurya Empire was built, ensuring stability and prosperity for generations. Chanakya believed that those who hesitate lose opportunities, while those who act at the right moment create success. He warned that procrastination leads to failure because time waits for no one. Success comes not just from knowledge but from the ability to execute plans at the right time.

Time is both the creator and the destroyer; waste it, and you fade; use it, and you rise.

Duryodhana, the prince of Hastinapur, had multiple opportunities to avoid the great war of Kurukshetra. He could have ended the rivalry with the Pandavas by offering them just five villages, as requested by Lord Krishna. Instead, he wasted time in arrogance and overconfidence, believing that he had the strength to win. Even when Bhishma, Vidura, and Lord Krishna advised him to act wisely, he hesitated and refused to take the right step. His inability to recognise the right moment to make peace resulted in his destruction, the loss of his kingdom, and the deaths of his family members.

Across the world, the pattern of human life follows a strangely similar route. A child is born, goes to school, moves to college, earns a degree, finds a job or starts a business, gets married, has children, raises them, sends them to school and college, and watches them get married and raise their children.

In the later years, the body begins to weaken, diseases arrive, and one day, life comes to an end. This cycle, whether lived with comfort or struggle, laughter or pain, richness or lack, moves along the same path for most people. Pleasure and suffering may vary from person to person, but the direction of life uses Kala in the same way, unless one dares to walk beyond this pattern.

Time is not bound to clocks, daylight, or nightfall; it flows the same—untouched by measure or means.

Rare are those who perceive Kala not just as a container for events but as a medium to search for meaning. They do not pass time, they live it. They question not the scriptures, but themselves. They use ancient wisdom not as superstition, but as a resource to understand life's deeper truths. They search for the origin of life, the foundation of their existence, the structure of their mind, the illusions that control them, and the invisible forces that influence everything around. These individuals do not spend their days completing tasks or following deadlines. They invest every moment in awareness, in self-inquiry, and in conscious living.

Such individuals use Kala not just for personal gain, but for inner growth and collective upliftment. They build businesses that inspire, create systems that serve, speak words that heal, and live in such a way that their presence becomes a guiding light for others. They are not interested in judgement, gossip, or approval. Their only concern is the wise use of time, knowing that every passing second is a step either towards awakening or ignorance.

Because they honour Kala deeply, they do not just find peace in death. Their life becomes timeless. They remain alive in the eternal memory of human history, not through statues or awards, but through the lives they touched and the light they left behind.

To live such a life is the highest way to honour time, not by merely following the same cycle again and again, but by using time to break the illusion, understand the self, and live with depth, purpose, and truth.

Exercise

This is a simple exercise. Pick any random day and, at night, tick in front of the statements below if you have done the activity. If not, mark it with (x). This will help you measure how well you are utilising Kala in its true sense.

- Did you experience any Klesha today?
- Did you spend time in Swadhyaya (self-reflection)?
- Did you do Aatma Vivechan (Self-analysis) on your past mistakes?
- Did you find multitasking possible and truly beneficial?
- Did your past memories (Smriti) disturb you today?
- Did your restlessness (Chanchalta) distract you in any way?
- Did you find it easier (Sahajata) to get angry or to stay peaceful?
- Are you satisfied with the way you spent your day?
- And have you made any plans to ensure that tomorrow is not wasted?

At the end of the day, count the checkmarks. By doing this daily, you will get a clear picture of how you manage time. You don't need a consultant or book to tell you how to improve; your answers will show you where you need to make changes.

Just try to be honest with yourself. If you notice anything going wrong in how you use Kala, commit to improving it. This simple act will help you utilise time more effectively than ever before.

Key Takeaways

Time is often seen but rarely valued. Though everyone speaks of time management, few truly practise it. Time is equal for all, yet only the wise use it well. Many realise its worth only during loss or urgency. History, mythology, and success stories show that those who respected time rose, while those who delayed fell behind. Real-time management is about inner awareness and action. Doubt and delay steal chances, while timely action shapes destiny and creates lasting impact.

Afterword

The Game of Choice

Destiny of Decisions

सुखदुःखे समे कृत्वा लाभालाभौ जयाजयौ।
ततो युद्धाय युज्यस्व नैवं पापमवाप्स्यसि।।

One of the most valuable shlokas from the Bhagavad Gita (2.38.15), Lord Krishna advises Arjun to make a conscious choice to perform his duty without attachment to the outcomes. By maintaining equanimity in the face of dualities like pleasure and pain or success and failure, one exercises the power of choice to act righteously, transcending personal biases and desires. This shloka emphasises that true freedom lies in choosing to act with detachment and dedication to one's duty.

Each choice is a thread in the fabric of fate.

Imagine if Duryodhana had stood in Arjun's place on the battlefield of Kurukshetra, listening to Lord Krishna's wisdom with an open heart instead of drowning in arrogance. Imagine if Ravana, the greatest devotee of Lord Shiva, had used his immense power to protect righteousness rather than abducting Sita and sealing his fate in flames. Imagine if Kansa had embraced Lord Krishna with love and devotion instead of feeding his soul with hatred and vengeance, if he had seen in Lord Krishna not as an enemy but the divine child meant to bring light into the world.

What if Hiranyakashipu, instead of trying to crush his own son's devotion, had accepted Prahlada's faith in Lord Vishnu? What if Manthara had never poisoned Kaikeyi's heart with jealousy? Imagine a world where Hitler had chosen peace over war, where he had seen Jews as brothers rather than enemies. What if Bin Laden, instead of becoming a symbol of terror, had used his engineering skills to build a prosperous nation, to serve his people, to leave behind a legacy of creation rather than destruction?

All of this could have been possible if only they had made the right, meaningful, and Dharma-based choice.

A choice to stand with humanity, to rise above their weaknesses, to be remembered as legends of wisdom instead of villains of history. They had the power to change their fate, to shape a glorious destiny, to turn their karma into something noble and divine. But they did not.

This is the power of choice. The strength of Dharma.

In our own lives, every day, every moment, we stand at a crossroads with two or more choices in front of us. These choices define our destiny. They shape the person we become. Through the choices we make, we either live a life of prosperity, peace, and joy, or we find ourselves trapped in doubt, hatred, anger, and ego.

It is easy to choose hesitation and protect a so-called image or to choose courage and showcase our true capabilities for the betterment of society.

To choose stability and calmness or to react and create Klesha (conflict), the suffering that arises from uncontrolled emotions. In every aspect of life, there is always a choice. What truly matters is the awareness that we have these choices in front of us before we make any decision.

Those who do not see both sides of a choice often make decisions under the influence of doubt, conflict, lust, greed, or whatever emotion is ruling their mind at that moment. The basic awareness that we have a choice makes us wiser, allowing us to analyse, reflect, and make a decision that aligns with our true path.

A choice should not be made based on the need for validation, Adharma, or to pretend to be someone who has sacrificed something. It must be made in alignment with the present moment's requirement, one's aspirations, keeping Dharma at the centre, and without degrading own karma.

The poor have limited choices, while the rich are surrounded by endless options—from food to clothes to luxury. But these are only external matters. What remains the same for all is the choice to remain peaceful inside, to stay calm in moments of pain and disturbance, and to keep the ground reality in mind.

It is often seen that the poor aspire to be rich. Across the world, almost 80 per cent of people are chasing wealth, yet they end up spending very little of it. Meanwhile, the rich make choices to live in luxury, often without realising the role of fate, Dharma, and karma in placing them where they are.

Many among them believe their wealth is solely the result of their intelligence and skills. No doubt, these qualities play a crucial role in success, but there are deeper forces at work, forces that determine who get what and why.

In much of life, choice escapes us,
yet where it exists, we often turn away.

The very first choice a person must make is to accept themselves just as they are, exactly how nature has designed them. The moment we start changing our true selves, we unknowingly open doors that lead us away from experiencing life in its fullest and most natural form. The more we try to alter ourselves to fit into expectations, illusions, and comparisons, the more we drift away from the joy of simply being.

However, the greatest choice a human being can ever make is to remain conscious, to become a witness to life as it unfolds, and to embrace the present without resistance.

People often fail to realise that they have a choice, not because they lack the ability to choose, but because hesitation clouds their vision. Hesitation keeps them trapped in overthinking, constantly analysing situations instead of acting upon them. It does not allow the mind to be silent and calm, which is necessary to clearly see things. The very nature of hesitation is to create confusion, to keep people stuck between yes and no, pulling them in different directions without letting them take a firm step forward.

Making a hard and wise choice requires something extra—patience, determination, and the willingness to step beyond comfort. But hesitation convinces people that it is easier to wait, to delay, and to avoid the struggle. It whispers that the right path is too difficult, that taking action might lead to mistakes or unfavourable outcomes, that it is better to stay where they are instead of walking into the unknown.

Humans naturally seek easier paths. They want quick results, instant answers, and life to unfold exactly as they wish, without discomfort or delay. But life does not follow our preferences. It unfolds through time, effort, and silent tests of patience. Wise choices often come wrapped in struggle and uncertainty. They demand clarity, courage, and discipline. Yet, instead of stepping forward, many choose to hesitate because it feels safe. It offers a temporary escape from the pressure of decision-making. Thus, they remain where they are, waiting, doubting, fearing, confusing, hesitating, while life quietly moves ahead without them. Moments slip by, opportunities vanish, and what 'could have been' is lost to time.

Hard work demands discipline, consistency, and the ability to stand your ground when things get tough. But most people are unwilling to go through that struggle. They jump from one goal to another, hoping to find something that requires less effort and gives quicker results. Every time they face challenges or see obstacles, they convince themselves that, perhaps, this is not the right goal and move on to something else.

Limitations are merely walls built by our minds; in reality, they rarely exist beyond thoughts.

The endless switching and fear of deep commitment keep them unnoticed and unsatisfied. Instead of walking the long road to mastery, they keep taking shortcuts that lead nowhere. In the end, success does not belong to those who chase every new opportunity, but to those who pick one path and walk it with determination, no matter how hard and delayed it gets.

The legendary actor Heath Ledger, who played the role of 'Joker' in the *Batman* movie, did not just act—he became the character. He locked himself in a hotel room for over a month, isolating himself from the world—no mobile, no internet, no distractions—just him and the silence. In that solitude, he practised calmness, immersed himself in contemplation, and deeply analysed human nature. This was not just preparation; this was dedication in its purest form. He was not looking for shortcuts, nor was he rushing to the stage. He was diving into the depths of the role, absorbing every emotion, understanding every shade of madness, pain, and chaos that made the

Joker so unforgettable. He knew that true art was not about pretending in acting; it was about living the truth of the character with consciousness.

**The greatest choice is to grow within;
the poorest is to prove you have.**

Think for a moment about the people you deeply care for. Imagine if they had made a different choice at a crucial moment in their life, a choice that could have spared them from sorrow, a choice that could have saved them from feeling lost, a choice that could have brought them peace and happiness. Can you see how just a simple decision could have changed everything for them?

Now, reflect on yourself. If only you could go back and undo some choices, correct the moments that led to pain, rewrite the past with the wisdom you have now. But that is not how life works. The past is untouchable, unchangeable, no matter how much we replay it in our minds.

So, instead of dwelling on regrets or imagining a different past, return to the present. The only thing you truly have is this present moment, right now, and the choices you make today will shape the days to come. Do not let your present become another regret in the future. Choose wisely. Choose consciously. Choose in a way that allows you to live without looking back with sorrow.

Choice is the real superpower that humans possess. It is the force of Dharma that shapes destiny, the unseen hand that turns suffering into strength, and the key that unlocks a life of meaning.

If life has a true synonym, it is choice. Some equate it with wealth, while others dissolve it in endless contemplation.

Prince Siddhartha had everything a man could desire—luxury, wealth, a powerful kingdom, and a life of endless comforts. Yet, something within him knew that there was more to life than fleeting pleasures. He chose to leave behind the palace, to walk into the unknown, to find the meaning of existence. His search led him to enlightenment, and he became the Buddha, the light that continues to guide millions. Just like him, Mahavir, too, renounced everything, choosing a path of deep meditation and spiritual awakening over the temptations of power and material success.

Emperor Ashoka was once one of the most ruthless conquerors the world had seen. His empire stretched far and wide, built on war, bloodshed, and destruction. But then came the battle of Kalinga, where thousands lay dead, the land soaked in the cries of the innocent. As he walked through the battlefield, something inside him shattered. In that moment, he had a choice to continue ruling through violence or to change his path forever. He chose Dharma over bloodshed. He turned away from war and became a force of peace, spreading wisdom, kindness, and non-violence across the world.

Each of them stood at a crossroads where they could have let circumstances define them. But they did not. They made a choice, a conscious decision to rise above pain, to break the chains of hesitation, and to walk towards something greater than themselves.

Choice is what makes a person a hero or a tyrant, a leader or a lost soul, a legend or just another name in history. Life does not decide for us. We do. And the choices we make today will shape the world we live in tomorrow.

People have the choice to be thankful, to embrace gratitude and fill their hearts with positivity, or to complain about everything and drain their energy. The words they speak can either bring people together, weaving bonds of love and understanding, or they can separate, leaving wounds on others' hearts that may never heal. People have the choice to turn their dreams into reality through courage and consistency, or they can live in the illusion of dreams, wrapped in hesitation and inaction, watching life slip through their fingers like sand. People have the choice to rise above their ego, lust, greed, jealousy, and anger by recognising these forces within, or they can remain slaves to their weaknesses. People have the choice to extend a helping hand, to lift someone up, to purify their karma, or they can mock those in pain, speak ill of others behind their backs, assassinate the character of achievers, in return, collecting the worst karma imaginable.

Similarly, they have the choice to be a listener (Shrota) or a speaker (Vakta), to live in the present moment or remain trapped in the regrets of the past and the worries of the future. They can earn and accumulate wealth endlessly or use it for something meaningful. They can choose to enjoy life, to embrace joy, or to drown in endless worry. They can take care of their health or let their body suffer from neglect. They can stay silent in reflection or snooze through life without a sense of purpose.

In the end, it all comes down to 'choice'. Every moment, every action, every thought, every word is a choice. And it is only these choices that shape the life a person will live. Nothing else.

Growth and decline, Dharma and Adharma, doubts and clarity, good and bad, all arise from our choices.

Choices reveal their true power not when a person is struggling, but when they achieve success and material growth. The real test begins when life starts offering comfort, status, and recognition. In such moments, the choice to remain grounded becomes most difficult. Often, people allow pride and ego to take control. Wealth and success begin to change their thoughts, their tone, and their behaviour. Slowly, arrogance grows, especially towards those who once stood beside them during their early days—family, relatives, and old friends. Their attitude shifts overnight. They begin to label the struggling ones as failures and see themselves as the only winners. It is against the Dharma.

This is where the most important choice must be made—to stay humble or get lost in the illusion of superiority. Those who choose gentleness, humility, and grace in success grow far beyond material measures. Their human capacity rises to saint-like purity. This is a common picture across society, seen in every circle. Yet, it remains the biggest missed lesson.

Love, compassion, and empathy are the rarest and highest qualities one can carry. They are more valuable than all the wealth of the world. They are signs of a person who is truly alive, aware, and conscious.

Always remember: Family and relatives are not chosen by us—they are gifted by fate. They are not to be measured by their position or wealth, but to be treated with dignity, love, and equality. That is the mark of true choice.

Exercise

Take a pen and paper and write down one choice for each important aspect of life, including what choice you need to make to become rich, respected, famous, joyful from within, and most loved in society.

Now, carefully observe every choice you have written. Be practical and honest with yourself. Notice which choices are still waiting to be made and implemented in your life.

These are the decisions that, once acted upon, can help you achieve all that you desire as soon as possible.

Remember, it is not just about making any choice; it is about making the *right* choice, one that is true to your purpose, aligned with your values, and capable of shaping your life in the best possible way.

कालः गच्छति, जनाः तु न गच्छन्ति।

[Time passes, yet people remain unchanged.]

Acknowledgements

WITH FOLDED HANDS AND A HEART FULL OF LOVE, I BOW before my late father, Shri P. K. Sharma, whose gentle light still guides me to the eternal wisdom of the Mahabharata and the Ramayana. To my mother, Savita, whose quiet strength has been my shelter; my beloved wife, Samruddhi, whose unwavering love walks beside me; my children, Siddhant and Ira, who fill my days with joy; and my dear niece and nephew, Nidhi and Atharva, whose smiles brighten every moment.

I bow in deep respect to my spiritual guru, Dr N. K., whose wisdom has been a torch in the dark corridors of the mind, leading me ever closer to the inner light. My heartfelt gratitude flows towards Shri N. G. Bendale Sir, whose inspiring work environment nurtured this book.

To my dear companions in this sacred effort, Dr Nishant Ghuge and Dr Swapnil Kate, your presence and timely guidance have been like steady pillars, holding the structure of this work upright. My warm thanks to Mr Ashwin Sanghi, Dr Anand Ranganathan, and Prof V. Kamakoti for their thoughtful insights and kind encouragement. I am honoured beyond words by the gracious foreword penned by Hon'ble Cabinet Minister Mr Piyush Goyal, whose words have touched this work with a golden light.

To my esteemed publisher, the Hay House team, and Ms Sonali Pawar, I offer my heartfelt thanks for believing in the seed of this work and helping it blossom into the world.

And to you, my darling reader, I bow in silent gratitude. By choosing to open these pages, you breathe life into these words. Without your presence, they would remain like unopened flowers, their fragrance unknown.

May this book be as much a reflection of your inner journey as it is of mine. May it serve as a humble offering at the feet of the Divine, for in the end, all that we create is but His grace flowing through us.

Life's true wealth is found in discovery, not in possession, for we are born to explore, not merely to accumulate.

'The gateways to wisdom and knowledge are always open.'

Louise Hay